BEHIND THE POWER

YOU'RE NOT CRAZY
YOU ARE POWERFUL

ALLYSON ROBERTS

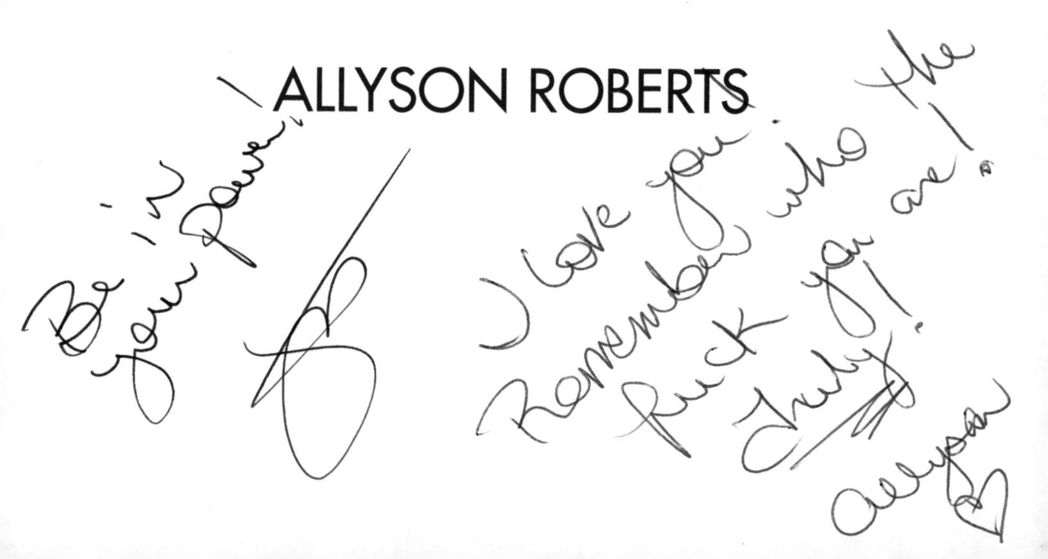

Behind the Power- *Volume 2*

You're Not Crazy, You Are Powerful

ISBN: 978-1-7375511-4-0 (paperback)
ISBN: 978-1-7375511-5-7 (eBook)

Library of Congress Control Number: 2022914381
Printed in Woodstock, Georgia, USA by Allyson Roberts.

For more information, visit AllysonRoberts.com.

TABLE OF CONTENTS

ACKNOWLEDGEMENTS

This book would not be possible without the dedication of each author to share their purpose with you. So, I'd like to acknowledge their time, effort, and energy required to pour their heart and soul into their story in order to help others heal.

I'd also like to shine a huge spotlight on Laura Lindsey for her coaching, editing, and devotion to this project. From the cover to the very last page, she immersed countless hours into this creation.

INTRODUCTION
ALLYSON ROBERTS

As I sit here writing this, I'm so grateful to the twelve women and one man who accepted the challenge to be coached on a deep level while writing about some tough stuff. In their writing process, they've accomplished three things. The first is to silence shame because shame loves secrets. When we are deep in our secrets, it's a breeding fest for deep shame and guilt to eat you alive. The second is that they stepped more deeply into their own authenticity. This allows them to show up their true selves, with fewer masks and more confidence than ever. The third reason is you. Yes, that's right. You are our reason for writing this. So that you know you are not alone.

You see, trauma is a very personal experience. Trauma to one person barely phases another. This is why it becomes such a big part of who we are and how we see the world. Trauma changes our DNA, as discovered by Dr. Vivian Rakoff. Epigenetics is the study of how behaviors and environments can cause changes to how genes function, and Dr. Rakoff's discovery is incredibly important to know because what it means is that parents who have unhealed trauma can pass it to their offspring. The beauty of trauma, however, is that healing those traumas breaks generational family "curses," and this is why we are here. It's also why we will be taking the stage in October at our second annual Behind the Power live event. Our mission is to heal ourselves and others from their trauma.

As you turn the pages and read through these very personal experiences, you're going to learn about the strength each of us possesses in our spirit to keep going. You'll walk through some dark places with each author as they share their heartbreak, shock, and unearthing moments. You'll see how their lives changed in an instant, and that it took years for each of them to develop the courage to finally face their pain. If any of this sounds familiar, it's because we are all more alike than we realize.

Each of these authors started out hiding behind words. Just like you, they were afraid of being judged, of hurting those closest to them who had no idea of the horrendous anguish they experienced. They were each hesitant to share certain decisions they've made on their life path as a result of their trauma. They all had the same question, "What if those I love decide to abandon me for finally sharing my truth?" It takes courage to break those chains.

As you dive into each story, I want you to know that each writer healed even more as they allowed the words to flow onto their pages. I want you to know that tears were shed as new realizations surfaced. I want you to know that they thought about you, and prayed that their bravery is contagious with you. That you can finally muster the strength inside of you to also heal what's been stopping you from having everything you want.

We've all been where you are right now. We know the pain of self-sabotage.

So, welcome to not being crazy. Welcome to understanding that your greatest pain can also be your most obvious power. Welcome to being safe in who you are, and what you've been through. We see you. We hear you. We get you.

As for me, this second year of *Behind the Power* has taken me to deeper levels in my own healing journey. (No, we are never "done.")

In January, I was invited to collaborate on another book, speak from a live stage at a BluTalk event, encouraged by my editor to write my own book, and a well-known production company reached out to me after a two-year hiatus to begin talks about a script again. *This all happened in January!* Not to mention getting geared up for this book, the Behind the Power Live Event in October, and coaching fifty clients.-

I woke one morning to my mother's voice asking, "Who do you think you are? Do you really think you can pull all of this together?"

I'm not going to lie, it took me down for a few days. The old feelings seep into my veins when I'm feeling the most vulnerable. I found myself questioning my ability to be a strong leader. "Who am I to do all of these great things?"

Laura Lindsey, the editor of this book and our Master of Ceremonies for Behind the Power, is also my social media manager. She encouraged me to start TikTok which is something I emphatically resisted at first. But, her reasoning, as usual, convinced me to take "the TikTok stage" and I'm so glad I did. It was support in the comments on my TikToks that supported me through my decision to continue on with everything on my list: the books, the script, the stages, and sharing my stories of years of childhood (and into my adulthood) abuse.

We each hold onto our pain until we don't anymore. Our pain can make us feel crazy. I'm here to remind you that you are NOT crazy, in fact, you're POWERFUL!

Thank you for being here. Thank you for taking this time for yourself. Each time you decide to do something for yourself, even as simple as reading a book, you create a ripple effect for healing in our world. So, thank you.

CHAPTER 1

COLLATERAL DAMAGE

ALLYSON ROBERTS

I was sitting on the beach in Florida eating ice cream purchased for me by a strange man sitting next to my mother a few towels away. I was in the sun, eating the melting mess in my hands as fast as I could. One because it was delicious and two because I was sticky. Being ten years old and alone with my mother was not a fun vacation. My dad and brother left a few days prior leaving me here with her. Little did I know that one of her many lovers would be joining us.

After the ice cream was in my belly, I stood and ran to the ocean. Daytona Beach is gulf coast water and the aqua blue waves were just what I needed. I jumped and squealed. The waves were bumping me as I tried to keep my balance. Finding my groove, I would catch the surf and ride it to shore. It was so fun!

During our visit, I met a girl named Sandy. We were the exact same age and liked the same music. She was the only child of proper parents. Her father was a psychologist and part-time minister. Her mother wore a lot of blue eyeshadow and fake blonde wigs. They were all adoring Elvis fans – the only thing we didn't have in common.

Sandy and I ran the hotel staff crazy while we were there. We rode the elevator dozens of times during the day just for fun. There was a slide at the pool which we climbed and slid down in every direction all day long. At night, we would jump in the pool and pretend like a shark was chasing us. Meeting her was a miracle.

Like all of my other friends' parents, Sandy's mom and dad saw through my mother from day one. They'd met us when my father and brother were still with us. Everyone had been introduced. Sandy's father and my dad spoke by the pool a few times, and my brother also met our new friends.

As soon as my dad and brother left for their return trip home, though, my mother invited her boyfriend to join us. It was awkward and I was confused. She'd kick me out of the hotel room for hours with no money and no plan. Sandy quickly caught on and she told her mom that my mother was sick. I didn't ask her to lie for me, she just did. As a matter of fact, I never asked for anything. Asking meant getting slapped or belittled … or both, so I learned to stay quiet.

When Sandy's mom agreed that I should stay with them the rest of the vacation so as not to catch anything from my mother, I was overwhelmed with feelings of safety. When I went to gather my things from the hotel room, I was so excited that I forgot to knock before placing my key in the door. I opened it quickly only to find this man on top of my mother. They were naked. I turned and ran from the room. I heard my mother say, "She will be fine. She's used to this," as the door closed behind me.

Sandy was waiting in the breezeway for me, and all I can remember is throwing my arms around her neck and sobbing. Looking back, I know she didn't know what to say or do. What ten-year-old kid knows how to handle that amount of stress?

We walked to her hotel room holding hands. Sandy was assuring me the whole time that her parents would know what to do. I didn't want to tell them what I saw, but I ended up confiding in them. I remember her parents sharing a long look without saying anything.

Finally, Sandy's mom stood and offered me some of Sandy's pajamas. Sandy's dad left the room and when he returned, he handed me a toothbrush and a coloring book with crayons. His eyes were red as if he'd been crying. Sandy's father had one more thing in his possession. Something I'll never forget. It was a map.

He walked over to one of the beds and spread out the map. He took a pen from his front shirt pocket and drew a line from my hometown to Chattanooga, TN. It wasn't far at all.

"Allyson, you are welcome at our home anytime. We only live just over an hour apart. It'll be fun. This way when we say our goodbyes tomorrow, you won't be sad."

Tomorrow? They were leaving. I felt my body go numb. *How was I supposed to survive the rest of my trip without them?*

Sandy and I hit the beach early the next morning. The sun was just rising. She shared how much she was going to miss me. I shared the same. We had become quick friends. She was, in fact, my only friend.

Little did I know how quickly my life would change.

When my mother found out that the McDonald family was leaving, she decided we should leave, too. I would find out years later that we left because my dad caught wind of what was going on in Florida. My mother looked scared. That was rare.

On our eight-hour drive home, all she said to me is that I better keep my "fucking mouth shut" if I knew what was good for me. I managed to fall asleep – my only escape. When we arrived home, the air was different.

It was early evening and the house was dark inside. My mother was yelling out to my father and brother, but her voice just echoed back. "Go find your brother."

My brother's bedroom was in our finished basement. When I went downstairs, my dad and brother were in my brother's bedroom. I could feel a definite shift. My dad ordered me to close my brother's door.

Once the door was secure, they each started drilling me about what happened in Florida. I so desperately wanted to tell them everything. I needed them to know I was on their side. But all I could think about was her threats in the car. She'd already shown all of us that she was physically violent. She hit us with anything she could find nearby. This included belts, clothes hangers, lamps, shoes, plates, and chairs. My mother wasn't well and we all knew it. In fact, she was evil just like her mother.

I froze. My dad showed his frustration. My brother begged me to say something. I hoped my eyes revealed my terror, but to this day I still don't know if either of them understood the terror inside of me.

"What do you think you're doing, Allyson? I told you to find your father and brother and you've decided, instead, to stand here and betray me. Fine, don't think I'll forget this because I won't."

Before I knew what was happening, my parents were in a huge fight. My brother grabbed me and took me upstairs. We sat in the kitchen chairs listening to the violence. When my dad emerged, he grabbed my brother and left. He didn't even look in my direction or speak a word to me.

It was my fault...again.

I would have chased after them, but honestly, I couldn't handle rejection anymore. What no one paid attention to is that this little girl was done. She was tired. She was hurting. She was confused. She just wanted to be loved and for everything to be okay. It was far from okay.

A few days later, my dad and brother were back home and my dad cornered me in my room. "Allyson, what happened in Florida? Please, darlin,' tell me."

The barbies in my hands came to life and I showed my dad what happened without saying a word. At first he didn't comprehend what I was doing, but he slowly caught on. "You saw this?"

I took my teen Barbie and had "her" write the word "Yes" on pink paper in front of me.

My dad stood and paced the room. "I'm going to fight for custody of you. Are you okay with that?"

I pointed to the "yes" I'd already written on my favorite paper.

He knelt down and held me close – something he hadn't done in years. When I was younger I would sneak from my bed and join him in his rocking chair every night. We'd watch the tail end of the news together and I'd always end up falling asleep in his arms. He'd wake me when the National Anthem played from the television right before service would disconnect to a snowy screen and white noise.

I'd find out years later that he stopped allowing me to sneak to him because my mother saw us one night and accused him of sexually molesting me. He was so terrified that she'd have him arrested, even though he was totally innocent, that he told me to stop visiting him after everyone else was sleeping. It was our special time and she knew it. The narcissist has to isolate its victim. It has no other choice.

Time passed and I overheard many of my mother's telephone conversations with her attorney as well as family members and friends. Even though she spoke in hushed tones, I knew the talks were about hurting my dad. She wanted revenge because my brother, who was then fifteen, had the freedom and choice to live with my dad.

When the day for court arrived, my mother woke me early and told me that I would be accompanying her to the divorce trial that day. She explained to me that I would be able to tell the jury who I wanted to live with and that, while the judge would make the final decision, whatever I said that day would hold a lot of weight in his decision.

While I brushed my teeth and put on the only clean clothes I owned (my mother had washed them the night before so I'd have them for court), I saw the pink paper with "Yes" that I'd shown my dad. He moved out the day after I confided in him, but I talked to him every day on the telephone after school.

The next morning, we rode the first half of the journey to the courthouse in silence. I sensed my mother was in deep thought. She broke the silence, "Allyson, who do you want to live with? It's important that I know."

I gazed out the passenger window frozen stiff. I despised everything about her. She knew I could see through her manipulation. I shrugged and refused to look at her.

Even though we were on a major highway and it wasn't safe, she pulled our car over to the side of the expressway. "Look at me, you little brat!"

The punishment for disobeying would be severe. It was in her tone. So, even though I'd rather have jumped out the car running for my life, I turned to face the person who hated me.

"You *will* say that you want to live with me! Do you understand?" It was a slow, exaggerated question where she made sure to prominently pronounce every syllable. It was sickening.

She glanced at her watch and pulled the car back into traffic. In her passive aggressive way, she put the pedal to the floor and put us in danger again. This was her usual behavior. As she sped, her words also raced.

"You will say that you want to stay in your school. Any question that's asked of you, you will tell the judge and all those people on the jury that you want to live with your mother."

I was frozen. My stomach was hurting. I said nothing, and I should've known better because my mother doesn't take the silent treatment well even though she's very good at dishing it out.

She shrieked, "If you don't say that you're living with me, you'll never see him again. I will make sure of that. And you can forget about seeing your sisters and brother, too. You selfish, fucking brat! Don't do this to me. I'm your mother. I'm the only one who's ever cared about you. Is this the appreciation you're going to show me now? Just sitting there, staring out the window like a retard, ignoring me? Maybe I should send you to live with your cousin, Rick, at the mental hospital."

We pulled into the parking lot. A police officer was standing next to his car. On cue, my mother flashed a big smile, swept her hair with her hand, and as she exited the car, "Hello, officer."

"Ma'am," was his only reply.

He and I exchanged glances. I wanted to scream, "She beats us! She hurts us! There's no food in the refrigerator at home. This is the first time I've worn clean clothes in weeks."

The unspoken words would form yet another shield around my wounded heart.

Once we were inside the courthouse, I saw my dad and grandmother immediately. It was clear that my dad had no idea I'd be coming to court that day. I could hear him pleading with my mother to take me back home and not put me through the trauma. He knew her all too well. She, of course, ignored him.

It came time for me to take my place on the stand. I swore on the bible I would tell the truth, but I knew I was going to lie.

"Do you want to live with your mother?" Her lawyer's booming voice hit me like a bullet.

I didn't answer.

"Allyson, please answer the court," the judge demanded.

"Yes," I barely whispered as my stomach dropped and for a moment my heart ceased beating.

I looked over at my dad who was weeping. He knew. I knew. My grandmother knew. But it didn't matter. Our knowing how evil she is didn't mean anything. All it did was make every decision hers.

Years later, I'm finally at a place where I can talk about this trauma without fearing my mother's retaliation. While she can spit venom and declare me a liar, the truth wins. She did have custody of me. My father was always afraid for me to live with him, even after I was of age to decide, he deterred it. The collateral damage was real.

The silver lining in all of this is that I broke the cycle of abuse. It wasn't done alone. My personal opinion is that we can't heal our cycles of dysfunction all by ourselves because we can't see our blind spots and that is where our "stuckness" lives – in the deep crevices that we can't see. So, at the young age of nineteen, homeless and pregnant with a son I knew I was placing for adoption to shield him from our toxic family, I got to work on myself. Sally, my psychologist, helped me see and comprehend the layers of narcissistic abuse I survived. She also helped me understand my parents' relationship.

Years later, I would discover that my dad wasn't my biological father and knew it but never told me. At first, I felt betrayed, but now I see how, even though I wasn't blood related to him, he still tried to save me from her. That's love. His love continues to heal me daily even though he left this world in 2017.

If this chapter has found you, and you're relating to any of this, what I want to say to you is that your parents' treatment of you is not your fault. Hurt people hurt people and, unfortunately, that can include an abuser's own child or children. It can take years to unravel the confusion if you attempt to try and heal on your own. This is why I created the *Unapologetic Power* program and the *Behind the Power* live event.. I want people to know that there's a better life waiting. You don't have to keep living in pain, and you're not crazy. You are powerful and there is a beautiful life waiting for you. I promise.

HELP IS HERE

Take three deep, cleansing breaths. The most effective way to do this is to count to four on the inhale, hold for the count of four, exhale to the count of four. Doing this three times calms down your nervous system. Note: If you're super anxious, you can do this breathing until you feel the release in your body.

Next, set an intention for your day. How do you want to feel when you lie down in your bed tonight? What do you want to have accomplished? Be very specific with your intention.

Now, ask yourself, what do I need to think to get me to this goal? Some examples are: I can do this. I want this for myself and so I will be the change I want to see. Hint: You must believe the thought or it won't work.

If your bed isn't made, go and make it. I know this sounds so simple, but studies have shown that accomplishing something very first thing in the morning has a positive ripple effect throughout the day.

As you go through your day, set small intentions for each hour. Make a promise to yourself. Example: Walk in place for 1000 steps. Journal instead of scrolling social media. Then, commit to the intention. If you stray from it, pay attention to what you're thinking.

Last, at the end of your day, look at the day's events. What outside circumstances happened that threw you way off course? How did you feel by not accomplishing something? Just the opposite, how did it feel to knock something out of the park?

If you follow these simple steps every single day, your life will look completely different in a year. Why? Because you will have accomplished three-hundred-sixty-five days of something instead of many days of nothing. You will have built brand new neurotransmitters taking you down a brand-new path. You see, you can't change your outside world until your mind changes. And that doesn't happen all by itself. You are your mind. Become the boss of it.

I'm offering these resources because the best gift I ever gave myself is admitting that I needed help. I still do this for myself. Also, if you are used to doing everything on your own, and not having like-minded people who understand your pain and who genuinely want to connect with you, then not only will your life improve by asking for what you need, but you'll also finally be surrounded by people who get and understand you.

I see you! I hear you. I love you.

YOUR SPECIAL GIFT

You're not crazy, you're powerful.

It's your time! Just decide that NOW is when you're going to finally shift into the greatest version of yourself and let's do this!

Here is a free gift for you. It's your reward for diving into this book, opening yourself to possibility, and laying the foundation for you to become THE best version of YOU! I get it, too. It's scary, and that fear is a gift. Do you know why? Because your feelings of fear mean that you're trying something new. Congratulations!

This guided meditation is focused on the younger version of you. That part of you that decided a long time ago that you're not enough, you're not worthy, and therefore need outside approval and validation. Ewww! That energy is gross, and honestly, because you're reading this, I know that it's an energy that no longer serves you. It's an energy that isn't even part of who you are becoming. So, it's time to go back and rescue that little person who is so powerful that they made up a bullshit story about not being enough so that their pain would make sense. Why? Because it's a lot easier to blame ourselves than blame two parents who are supposed to be perfect and never do anything wrong so that we feel safe.

The brain is crazy powerful!

So, your lack of enough-ness was a story you made up about yourself or confirmed for yourself if someone conveyed it to you. So, it, therefore, is a choice you can reverse by deciding you are, in fact, enough! That's where this meditation comes in.

Please take fifteen minutes, sit or lie down, and go on this journey with me.

Go to https://www.allysonroberts.com/specialgift to access the special Guided Meditation. Use the password **Powerful2022** to access the page.

Or scan the QR code below to access the page.

Once you've listened, I'd love to hear your feedback. You can also schedule time to speak with me about how to work with me so that I can help you learn how to BECOME the most powerful version of yourself. Just scan the QR code provided below and pick a time to meet with me.

I'm looking forward to meeting you!

All my love and support,

Allyson

You're worth it
Say yes to you!
Anna Davis

CHAPTER 2

UNPROCESSED GRIEF

ANNA DAVIS

The regular phone call with Mom and Dad was far from regular that day. I answered, "Hey! How are things?" Both of them were on the phone, which was unusual. Mom usually was on the line first, then Dad would get on briefly.

"Hallelujah! We got an answer from the doctors as to what is causing your mom's symptoms!" My dad rejoiced.

"Praise Jesus, we know what is happening!" Mom chimed in sounding equally relieved. All I could register were the words Lou Gehrig's disease and fatal, yet my parents seemed so happy because they had an answer. I could not comprehend their reaction.

Last year it was Dad being diagnosed with lung cancer. My husband and I already had plans to visit our families and introduce our almost one-year-old son. Dad's diagnosis came just before our trip. He was getting treatments before and during our time there. He actually looked really good, which was nothing like his first bout with cancer shortly after our move to Kansas when I was twelve. That time, he had surgery to remove a lymph node, then radiation that left him weak, his skin burned and raw. He was declared cancer-free back then after the brutal treatments that seemed to last a lifetime. Now, this time around, the treatments and side effects seemed mild. He was told at the end of these treatments the cancer was in remission.

Growing up I thought of Dad as healthy and Mom as sickly. There was no discussion with either me or my sister about her health. Somehow we just knew that her physical health was not optimal, leading to a hysterectomy at a young age which is why we were both adopted. When I was fifteen years old she had a hip replacement that left one leg a bit longer than the other, giving her a pronounced limp, which added a visual aspect to these lifelong issues.

Even though I considered Dad the healthy one, cancer was not his first health crisis. I was seven years old and we had just moved for the second time in just a couple of months when Dad was hospitalized with pneumonia. I remember being so scared for my Daddy when he was away in the hospital, hearing adults talk about how he almost died because one lung was completely full of fluid and the other was half full. Throughout my life I can remember all of these health crises for both of them, where they had treatment options and they always seemed to help, but not this time. There were no treatment options for Mom with Lou Gehrig's Disease. The deterioration in her health would keep progressing until her body gave out.

Mom wanted to visit me, my husband, and my son in the Keys before traveling would become too difficult. She came at Easter along with my father. We got them a small apartment on the ground level that could accommodate her wheelchair. We had such a wonderful visit with them. It felt wonderful seeing my son laughing and playing with his grandparents. I wish I had known it was going to be the last holiday we could spend together. Shortly after returning home to Kansas, Dad had his one-year check-up with his oncologist. The cancer had returned, but this time it was also in his brain.

I flew up to Kansas with my young son to help in any way I could. I was able to take my Dad to a few chemotherapy treatments. He was doing extremely well, all things considered. He was caring for Mom day in and day out without any help, on top of taking care of himself and all of his medications. Sadly I could only stay for a week before going back to work. His treatments ended soon after that trip, but the tumors remained. Even if they had reduced in size, there was nothing we could do – the tumors kept growing. He had received the maximum amount of radiation, meaning that soon he would begin to deteriorate little by little, after which he would not be able to care for Mom or for himself. Watching this happen to my parents was heartbreaking beyond words.

My husband and I had many discussions about the care they would both need, and we knew they would want to remain together; no separate facilities or housing. My husband suggested they come live with us, and after pitching the idea to them, my parents agreed to make the move down to Florida. We found our new, ground level home, and I felt really good about Mom and Dad committing to this change.

When we bought the house we needed a down payment, so we took a second mortgage on our ½ duplex and we were able to get the mortgage for the new home. We immediately started renting the duplex when we moved out. We were feeling financial anxiety going from one to three mortgages. We were both raised to believe you meet your financial responsibilities no matter what, and we still felt we had made the right decision.

Mom and Dad spent the holidays at their home in Kansas, knowing it may be their last together. Dad had another experimental treatment scheduled during the week between Christmas and New Year's Day, and unfortunately my husband and I had no idea of this until after it was done. This procedure involved direct radiation into the tumors in the brain by laser, even though we had been told his body couldn't handle any more radiation. Since we were not present when the procedure was explained to Dad and Mom, I don't know what they were told about what the immediate results could be. The main part they heard and told us about later was that this was a way to extend Dad's life by a few months.

My sister called that day in a panic. She sounded winded just trying to say the words, "Oh my God! You have to come. I don't know what to do! It's awful! Dad is a mess! He can't take care of himself and definitely can't take care of Mom!" I was shocked to hear this; we had spoken to Mom and Dad on Christmas day and they both sounded great, but of course there was no mention of the upcoming procedure. I told my sister I would get there as soon as I could. My next call was to my boss.

"My dad is in really bad shape, my parents need my help now."

"No!" she snapped back. "You must give your fellow employees a week's notice before you can leave." I was absolutely gut punched. I froze for several moments feeling panicked and told her I would be leaving on emergency leave in one week. My husband volunteered to go be with my parents. He called his boss, who I overheard on the phone saying, "Go take care of your family, take as much time as needed. Family comes first." I still remember how that only emphasized the belittlement my boss made me feel. My husband was on the next flight to Kansas, but by the time he arrived my dad's brother and his wife were there to help, too; the situation was that dire. Dad's medical conditions had changed so drastically and rapidly that he needed round-the-clock nursing care. To make matters worse, my mom also needed the same type of care. They decided to stay together in Kansas. My husband and uncle took control of things and found a nursing home where Mom and Dad could be together and receive the care they needed. By the time I arrived a week later most of the arrangements were finished despite there being many financial matters to figure out.

My family barely spoke to me. I felt so judged by them. I remember there was a moment in this chaos when my uncle turned to my husband and said condescendingly, "You two picked a fine time to move away." He reminded my uncle that we had moved ten years ago, not recently. By the end of the week Mom and Dad were moved into the nursing home. The rest of the family was so cold to me the whole time I was there. Looking back I wish I had quit my job on the spot when my boss made me give a week's notice for an emergency. The family believed I was more concerned about my job than Mom and Dad. The truth was that I was terrified. Fear was constantly whispering, "What if?" in my ear. What if we can't pay all our bills? What will happen when Mom and Dad are gone? What if this traumatizes our young son? What if I lose control over this situation? I wasn't living at that point, I was just existing day to day.

Just a few months later Dad's body gave up and he was gone. I was overwhelmed with grief. We flew to Kansas for his funeral where, once again, I felt no support, comfort, or sympathy from anyone in the family. No one asked how I was feeling or even offered a hug. I felt ashamed and rejected. Just as Dad's service was ending we got word that Grandma Baker, my mom's mom, had been taken into the hospital and wasn't expected to be with us much longer. We all jumped in cars and headed up to see her in the hospital in Wichita. She offered me love and support even though she was also dying. She passed away a week later, after we were already back home. We were unable to come back for her funeral, which meant more disapproval from the family, even though the money we were trying to save was so we could make a trip to see my mom. Hurricane Georges changed those plans. We had flood damage to the entirety of the house. The additional financial burden of rebuilding our home left us unable to afford the travel expenses to Kansas.

When we finally had room on the credit cards for travel expenses, I spoke to Mom and told her of the planned trip in a few weeks. She sounded so happy to hear I could finally come see her, and it was a huge relief on my end too, but I was also feeling overwhelmed with guilt that I was so far away and not able to be there for her. Just a few days later my aunt called.

"Come now, your mom has taken a serious downturn." I was on the next available flight to Kansas. I arrived less than twelve hours later, but I was too late. My sister picked me up at the airport and she told me in the car that Mom had passed. She was gone and I was too late. I wasn't prepared for that at all. I was sure I would be able to say goodbye.

I stayed with my sister while I was there, but felt, yet again, like I was all alone. She was cold and distant, leaving me alone most of the time and staying in her room. Mom's service was a few days after I arrived, and it was a lot like Dad's service where I felt completely isolated. At least at Dad's service I had my husband there for support, but because of how abruptly everything happened, there was no time for my family to make it – I had to face this loss completely alone. None of my mom's siblings or friends offered me any comfort or support. Years later I learned that all of Mom's siblings and their families got together for a barbecue at her brother's place, the same day as her funeral. My sister and I were not invited even though my sister lived just minutes away. I felt so disconnected and unwanted. *Did my aunts and uncles not think of us as "real" family members because we were adopted? What had we done to deserve this kind of treatment?*

Just six weeks after Mom's passing my boss fired me. I was away from the toxic work situation, but I was really scared about keeping the bills paid, paired with the fear of being all alone with no parents now. I had always relied on Mom to keep me in the loop of all the happenings with the family, but now that she and Dad were gone the family made little effort to keep us included.

I got a job working at a bar in a restaurant. Industry practices have made it normal for a bar job to include a free shift drink, and that gave me an excuse to use alcohol to numb out instead of processing my feelings of loss and grief. The outside appearance I gave was that everything was just fine, but inside I was a mess. Unresolved grief was twisting inside me.

One day I had a table of tourists from the same area as my uncle. I told them I was familiar with the very small town they were from in Indiana, that my favorite uncle lived near there.

"Who is your uncle?" they asked. When I told them his name their faces fell.

"We are 99% sure that he passed away last month." When I got home I googled his obituary and found out that it was true. No one in the family had ever bothered to let us know. I realized then I had no family except my son, husband, and his extended family. This magnified my feelings of abandonment and isolation. All of these losses happened so close together and each time I just pushed the feelings down. I didn't let myself feel the feelings. I just bottled them up inside. As expected, using alcohol to numb out did not always work, and sometimes it would amplify how extremely sad and depressed I felt. Instead of dealing with those feelings, I would sober up and go back to keeping everything inside and projecting to the world that I was just fine.

While there is an actual process to grieving, it was very different for me because I was experiencing so many losses and so quickly; I had no emotional space or time to process and heal before the next thing would happen. When I did try and look at my feelings, it was uncomfortable and I just wanted to go back to numbness. For me, the unresolved grief eventually brought me to anger. Although I was not aware at the time, I was stuck in a triggered state of anger; it was there under the surface all the time and the smallest thing would release it. Mostly the anger was directed at myself, but unfortunately it did get misplaced on others, too. Now looking back I can recognize all the self-sabotaging behaviors, but at the time I had no idea what I was doing.

By ignoring my feelings and keeping them hidden, especially from myself, they festered inside causing both physical and emotional pain. I suffered for many years and had, for the most part, decided that this was how my life was now. I was looking externally for solutions to the pain. I eventually stopped working in restaurants/bars and my drinking on a regular basis stopped, but pushing my feelings down and reacting in anger continued.

Reflecting on this healing journey I'm on, the beginning of the healing started for me when I was introduced to Tai Chi. It has been described as a moving meditation, and I found my mind and body were calmed by my practice of Tai Chi. Last year the final pieces to move my healing forward came when I joined Allyson Roberts in her Unapologetic Power program. The teachings from her classes and one-on-one sessions with her have brought me so much awareness. My blind spots have had spotlights placed on them, giving me the tools I needed for true healing. I am just getting started! I know now, I can keep growing and healing for the rest of my life.

PATH TO YOUR POWER

I spent so much time pretending I was just fine. I was keeping my feelings shoved down, never allowing myself to feel them. I thought if I just pushed through, things would eventually get better. That was the furthest thing from the truth. Instead I was marinating in shame and guilt, second-guessing every decision I made. The pain showed up in every part of my life. I was miserable, but most of the time I put on a happy face. I cried many times when I was alone, then shoved the pain and sadness aside to get on with life the best I knew how.

When I was betrayed by people I thought were my friends, I sought out a counselor. She recognized the anger I was holding onto inside. The pain, anger, and fear were all present, as well as shame and guilt. They continued to fester inside and showed up in all parts of my life.

I always struggled with questions about my adoption. I always knew I was adopted, but that was all the information I had. Why? That was always the question. Why was I given up for adoption? I had no information about my origins. The worst thought to arise when I was in the depths of despair was a reminder that I was "unwanted" since before I was born. Which was not true, my adoptive parents wanted and loved me. But with both of them gone and the rest of the family with no interest in including me, it was easy to sink into despair and feel so unwanted and completely worthless. Feelings of worthlessness caused so much pain emotionally, mentally, and physically. The physical pain at times seemed unbearable and I did look for solutions to my physical pain. Being connected to nature was always the best time for me, even when at my lowest points. Walking, biking, snorkeling, or even a boat ride. The movement helped get me out of my head.

Several things happened at about the same time. My son had left for college, I started working at a natural health food store, and I started the practice of Tai Chi. With my son off at school, I wasn't busy and distracted helping to support him. I finally started to pay attention to myself and what I might need. I started the Tai Chi class and was hooked. I was also really loving my job, where I was learning to heal myself and others with the natural bounty of Mother Earth.

These things were a jump start to my healing process that was basically stalled out for such a long time. All the years of keeping my feelings inside had taken its toll. Tai Chi was so calming to my mind, body, and spirit. Working at a natural food store brought so much learning about food and how it can harm you or heal you. The connections made there to people would come back around and bring me the tools I'm using now to get deep healing. I'm learning to take back my power, stop beating myself up, and most importantly for me, to not bury my feelings.

You cannot heal if you bury your feelings. You must acknowledge them and let yourself feel them. Writing them out in a journal or brain dumping all the thoughts when you have been triggered is key to understanding and awareness. Once you get it down on paper examine those thoughts and feelings, get curious, be an observer of yourself. Ask yourself questions to better understand the feelings that are associated with your thoughts. Now take some time in meditation to process what you've learned.

Forgiveness is a must! You must forgive yourself as well as others for whatever it is that you've been holding onto. Forgiveness does not necessarily mean reconciliation. You're just letting the grudge go. As long as you hold onto the anger you're poisoning yourself and that poison will infect you in so many ways.

Taking a look back to your childhood is key. Even if you had "perfect" parents, trauma can still happen. Did you move around a lot? Did you lose grandparents? Did you experience a natural disaster? I always thought of trauma as something really horrific happening to you such as abuse, or a fire burning down your home. Trauma can be different for everyone. Trauma is something that happened to you that changed the way you viewed the world. For true healing you must heal that wounded inner child. When you let your inner child feel safe, your adult self will also feel safe. Once you heal these stories from your past, you move forward in a new direction not repeating the toxic patterns of your past.

For me, the key is self-worth. I still struggle sometimes with feeling worthy. That voice will creep in bringing self-doubt with it. Self-care is key to feeling your self-worth. That looks like taking time to just breathe, calming your mind, and letting yourself just be. Making promises to yourself and keeping them. Setting healthy boundaries. Getting your thoughts on paper.

I found out I am much more powerful than I ever knew. And believing in myself is the key to my continued growth and healing.

ABOUT

Anna Davis is a fighter for the underdog. She has worked on many campaigns, bringing awareness to social justice issues for people, animals, and environmental issues. She helped to organize the local March for Our Lives in her town, and is always looking for ways to make a difference. She has several rescue animals in her care. She volunteers as an instructor for Tai Chi and also serves on the Branch Council for her Tai Chi organization.

She lives in the Florida Keys with her husband of forty years. They have one grown son. She loves gardening and making special fairy gardens using repurposed items. She's passionate about sharing the message that physical healing is possible with plant-based whole food nutrition. She helps people "bridge the gap" to complete whole food nutrition as a health and wellness advocate with Juice Plus business. She loves to travel, especially to see her son.

To work with Anna in your journey to health, visit her website: annadavis.juiceplus.com.

shine bright!
much love,
Audra Zimpel

CHAPTER 3

FROM ACTING TO LIVING

AUDRA ZIMPEL

Have you ever had suicidal thoughts? It's a bold question, isn't it? It's certainly not something you ask someone you just met. And, I imagine, I'm most likely meeting you for the first time here on these pages. So, forgive me for the shocking nature of my opening here, but really, wouldn't it be helpful if we all talked about this issue more? I mean, even if you yourself haven't considered suicide, odds are, sadly, very high that someone close to you has. I have. Here's a bit of my story.

In my early thirties, I was living in LA, trying–and failing–to be a successful actress. I spent my time driving all over LA, taking classes, working temp jobs, performing in a few fantastic plays, but mostly just CHASING the "big break." Though I LOVED performing (the thrill of performing before a live audience was wildly intoxicating to me, what a RUSH) it wasn't my passion for acting that was ultimately motivating me to do all of this exhausting, and many times heart-breaking, running around. Not at all. The real reason I was doing all of this? To stop feeling worthless.

The fact that I felt worthless would have come as a shock to a lot of people who knew me. I appeared to be "miss perfect." Always happy, always positive. Nobody knew about the putrid feelings of worthlessness stuffed deep inside me. My thinking was that if I could be a successful actress, that would mean I was worth something; that I could banish the awful feelings that gnawed at me every single day. I would finally be worthy of love. And I would finally feel safe. That's the story my seven-year-old self had created. That's the story that was running through me. My seven-year-old self was in charge of my life and she was desperate for outside validation.

Who exactly did this little girl want validation from? And why? Everyone. She wanted everyone to like her. She wanted everyone to think she was a nice person. And she really wanted to make her family proud of her. She wanted these things even if it meant ignoring the voice inside that wanted something different: an authentic life. A life in which her unique needs mattered. Why? She was terrified. Terrified of this world and terrified that she was a bad person.

When I was seven years old, I was picked up from school early but didn't know why. My beautiful, hard-working mom gathered my two brothers and me in the kitchen, took a deep breath, and said something that couldn't possibly be true… except it was. "Your dad took his life this morning." It didn't feel real. It felt like a nightmare. My body froze. Shame and guilt flooded me.

I felt responsible. Then the thoughts began, *I'm not good enough. I didn't do enough to make my Daddy stay. I'm a terrible person.*

On that awful day in April 1980 when my father's battle with depression became too much for him, my seven-year-old self didn't understand the situation. But she could feel the devastating sadness and the deep shame stemming from the stigma attached to the way he died.

On that day, something deep inside decided that to be safe in this horrific world, a world where my sweet, kind, handsome daddy could suddenly cease to exist, I have to manage the feelings of everyone around me. I have to make sure they're happy. I don't want anyone else to kill themselves. *If I can always be 'the good girl' and pleasing to people, I can remain safe.* This led to a young life filled with anxiety and inauthenticity about what I was feeling and thinking. I began hiding.

It started with always answering the question "How are you doing?" (shortly after my dad's death) with, "I'm doing really well." And smiling. I had noticed how uncomfortable talking about my dad's death made people, and the thought of making someone uncomfortable was way too painful and scary. So I lied. I noticed how it lifted people's spirits when I pretended to be "happy" and "fine." So I became an expert at appearing "happy" and "fine." And I continually ignored any feelings that didn't fit my chosen narrative of "Happy, good girl."

All of this hiding inevitably led to me feeling like an imposter. So even though I've had wonderful friends throughout my life, I've always had the nagging feeling that they didn't really love me. How could they? They didn't really know me. What I longed for most was genuine connection, but my coping mechanism of people-pleasing prevented me from ever truly having it.

Along with hiding, I began performing. Specifically, I competed in pageants and received a ton of validation from my mother, in particular, when I would do well. The whole family was pretty excited when I competed in a televised national pageant and placed third. It felt amazing! I genuinely loved so many aspects of competing. But it also felt like a strange kind of pressure. Something in me questioned if I would have their love and approval without the pageants. Did my family pressure me? No, and if they

had known I was feeling worthless deep down, I believe they would have been shocked and heartbroken. But how could they have known?
I was hiding.

Somewhere along the way, I decided that being a successful actress would mean I had permanent worth. So back to LA... After years of struggling to achieve success and fighting feelings of worthlessness, depression and anxiety had begun to consume me. Negative, critical self-talk was a constant occurrence in my head. The energy required to hide all of the darkness under the surface was draining me fast. My entire being began to feel like a ticking time bomb.

In one of my darkest moments, I was walking down the street to meet a friend at a nearby park. For the last few months, he had noticed a change in me and had grown increasingly concerned. He asked me to meet him to have an honest conversation about my state of mind. The truth was that I was falling apart. I was struggling to fight back not just tears but gut-wrenching sobs that had been shaking my body for three days. Vicious thoughts raced through my mind on a loop. *You're a complete failure. You're a loser. You're irresponsible. You're a burden on your family. You're pathetic. You're weak. You're an imposter. You're not pretty enough. You're too heavy. You're stupid. You're a coward. You'll never be successful. You're a terrible person.* The pain involved in getting dressed and leaving my room, much less leaving my apartment was excruciating. For someone who has never dealt with severe depression and anxiety, I'm sure this is very hard to understand. "I mean, you just get dressed and walk out the door. How hard can it be?" But as the saying goes, if you know, you know.

Before I knew it, a wave of darkness canceled out all the light. As I walked down the street toward the park, I started to imagine how easy it would be, and what a relief it would be, to just step in front of the speeding oncoming traffic. It didn't just seem like a relief. It

seemed like a really good idea. For that moment, my conscious mind, the mind that would never dream of inflicting the pain a suicide would cause my family and friends, had left the building.
How did I get here? What happened to me? How do so many of us get to this point? So many stories, so many reasons...but I've come to believe that a common thread in so many cases is feeling a lack of safety...and trading self-acceptance for that coveted feeling of safety. For me, losing my dad and burying my thoughts and feelings about it led to me feeling incredibly unsafe. To feel safe, I became an expert people-pleaser.

In a way, this worked tremendously well for me as a child. I could keep my scary feelings at bay if it meant that everyone around me appeared happy. I would do whatever it took to keep them looking happy. But eventually, I lost myself. As I grew up, I had a hard time identifying what my own needs, wants, and opinions were. I just adopted the ones I thought people wanted me to have. And of course, I constantly felt guilty about being an imposter. I doubted my connections to people. They weren't fully authentic because nobody knew the real me.

But there was a place where I was always my authentic self. As the only girl growing up in a house full of brothers and step-brothers, I spent a lot of time alone in my room. I clearly remember reading my children's bible, praying, and teaching myself to meditate without even realizing it. Alone in my room, I gave myself the space to be honest about how I was feeling about the loss of my dad.

I remember countless times that I would try to talk to him. "Daddy, I miss you. Why did you go away? I'm so afraid I'm going to forget you." I longed to talk to him. In the silence of meditation, I began to realize I had an intuitive gift, though I didn't know that's what it was called. The same feeling I had experienced hugging my dad while he was still with us flooded my heart. I sensed the love he had for me in the most beautiful way. It was wonderful! God allowed me to feel my dad's presence. My intuitive gift helped me to open up to receive and experience divine guidance profoundly. I experienced it as a deep, unshakable knowing that I was loved and I wasn't alone. Although, in the future, my mind would at times obscure the awareness of being divinely guided, I now know the guidance never left me. I'm convinced it was this guidance that kept me from stepping into oncoming traffic that day.

I'm so very grateful that I didn't end my life. There was healing in my future. And a wonderful husband and beautiful children. Joy, laughter, and peace. But guess what? There was also more hiding. My life-long habits of people-pleasing and hiding would be with me for many more years after leaving acting.

People-pleasing became my "go-to" coping mechanism. It went on for decades. What's interesting is that years ago, this was brought to my attention and, honestly, it made me defensive inside. Internally, I bristled at the thought that I was "people-pleasing" because I thought that meant I wasn't genuinely a nice person. And that seemed to threaten my very existence! How can I function in this world if I don't have the "safety" of being seen by others as a NICE person? You can probably see how the idea of being truly authentic goes out the window when the focus is to be perceived as a certain kind of person.

An interesting thing I've found about growth: It causes brand new layers of obstacles to show up. Case in point: A few years back, I became an intuitive coach. I began living my dream of being of service to help others find healing, joy, peace, and abundance in their lives. But when it came time to get the word out about my services, I froze. I again began to feel like I was going to be exposed as being a "bad" person. It made no sense. My clients were enjoying great success. But part of me was determined to hide.

For a moment, let's consider how much of the world is stuck in this very cycle. How many would-be healers are stopped by the fear that they're "bad" or "not good enough," "not worthy" or "an imposter." But there's a place inside us that knows the truth. But we deny ourselves access to this place by refusing to accept ourselves.

I had spent years seeking approval and acceptance from others, but what was missing was self-acceptance and love. That's why I was so externally focused; there was a huge hole inside where my self-acceptance belonged and I kept getting frustrated with other people for not filling it. This showed up in so many ways.

It showed up in my early years being married as trying to be the perfect wife, avoiding conflict at all costs even when it meant not speaking my truth. It showed up as a new mom, not admitting when I was feeling inadequate and needed support. And as a friend, it showed up as not admitting when something had hurt me. Because self-acceptance is necessary for living an authentic life, the joy was never full. The peace was never complete. The hole remained.

Did I know I was people-pleasing and hiding? No, for most of my life I had no idea. I often just felt isolated and extremely anxious in social situations. I felt empty and disconnected like nobody understood me. I felt sad and embarrassed. Ashamed. But I didn't know I was hiding. When I was people-pleasing, I just thought I was being a nice person, being generous and thoughtful. A whole new world opened up when I realized, through working with gifted therapists and coaches, that I was hiding and people-pleasing. I finally learned what it meant to accept myself. And I gained access to a new level of power and energy I had been depriving myself of my entire life.

Once I understood what people-pleasing was, I was still afraid that I'd find out I wasn't a nice person. What if I didn't have a nice bone in my body and had just been faking it all these years to feel safe?

I found out the opposite. When I dropped the people-pleasing, I deeply, genuinely connected with myself and others like never before. I did the most loving thing I could do: I let people have the space to have whatever thoughts, feelings, and opinions they wanted to have without trying to control them. What a concept! I no longer needed them to APPROVE of me, so I could freely give them the AUTHENTIC me. No expectations. Just the possibility of a genuine connection. And for me, the key to unlimited JOY.

PATH TO YOUR POWER

What has been most helpful to me in breaking the people-pleasing habit? As I contemplated this question, I realized my intuition had again saved me… What has been most helpful is embracing what my intuition has guided me to recognize as TRUE:

1. I am a creation of God and am therefore inherently worthy. No external validation needed.
2. God created me to be ME. I can fulfill my purpose in life only by being true to my authentic self.
3. What other people think of me is none of my business.
4. Attempting to control people's perception of me is not loving. I lovingly allow others to have whatever thoughts and feelings they choose.
5. Being my authentic self helps others do the same. We all have permission to SHINE!
6. I can be kind, compassionate, loving, and generous, AND create and maintain healthy boundaries.
7. I don't need to be perfect to be loved. Through being my authentic, imperfect self, I create the possibility for genuine connection.

8. If God approves of me, I'm good. No external approval needed.
9. I can honestly and kindly tell the truth about my thoughts and feelings.
10. I can fully accept and love my imperfect self.
11. I am safe and loved.

Do these eleven truths resonate with you? I invite you to tap into your intuition and see. Perhaps you will discover new ones, too. I would love to hear about your journey! Please reach out to me if you feel inclined to share. Wishing you joy and freedom as you break the people-pleasing habit and embrace the authentic, powerful you!

ABOUT

Having lived through a dark journey of clinical depression and emerged with more joy in her life than she previously could have imagined, Audra Zimpel is passionate about helping women find their way back to their radiant light. As an intuitive life coach, she excels at helping people grow with a powerful, yet gentle approach. She's a big believer in giving ourselves permission to shine through spirit-led self-care.

Get your free copy of *The Pink Pages*, a collection of empowering messages inspired by Audra's private coaching business. Claim your copy at https://www.audrazimpel.com/resources.

Have courage!
Michelle

CHAPTER 4

A JOURNEY BACK TO INNOCENCE

MICHELLE SULLIVAN

Let me tell you a story about how I went on a journey to rescue a younger version of myself, and before I do I want to say that this story contains trauma surrounding childhood sexual assault. Please read with care. My journey was a valiant one. It took courage. I knew that the time had come, after fifty-two years, for me to set out to heal something stolen from me at a very young and innocent age. Are you on a healing journey? My hope is that you can begin to recognize and embrace your own story as I share mine.

I came into this world in August of 1965. I've been told that I was a beautiful child with big blue eyes, curly red hair, and a smile that would melt your heart. I knew I was loved, wanted, and cared for. My parents were so happy that I was a part of their lives; their firstborn child. As I grew and developed, I became a curious little girl with a creative and imaginative mind. I loved to play with my dolls. I had a little play stove where I would take mini marshmallows and pretend to cook a meal for them. I pretended to be a momma. I modeled what was modeled for me. Without a doubt I was innocent, carefree, and I trusted everyone.

We moved to a beautiful rural part of Alabama when I was four. We had no close relatives nearby, so the opportunity to create another "adopted family" began. I remember just a few neighbors around this area. The community was spread out among cow pastures, mountain views, and wide expansive skies. I loved living there. By this time, I had a new playmate, a brother. We spent many hours each day playing outside and exploring the huge yard. I have memories of playing on our swing set, baptizing each other in our little plastic pool, and singing "We all live in a yellow submarine" at the tops of our lungs. It was a magical time. We roamed freely without any care or concern.

Up the hill from our house lived a widowed neighbor. She was a loving and caring person and she had influence in the community. I remember going to her house and eating delicious food at her little round table. My brother and I would play on her front porch often. I can still smell the sweet perfume of purple petunias on her porch on a cool summer evening. We were welcome there.

What I was not aware of was what was lurking in the shadows, behind her house. She had two brothers who lived on the property behind her. At this point I want to introduce you to "the thief." I call him that because of what he stole from me.

I don't have any recollection of what it was that drew me to the thief. He knew how to lure children. There was always something curious going on at his place. He knew how to groom children by offering things of interest to them and therefore gaining trust. What seemed to stick in my mind was that he would keep minnows in his bathtub. I thought that was so fascinating. He would invite other older children in the area into his home, often offering money for house cleaning. I was told this information as I connected with one of those children just this past summer as I was beginning the healing process. I have no way of knowing what else may have happened to the others. I become filled with sadness and rage when I think of how many more had been tricked by him.

At just four years old, I was sexually molested several times by the thief, and that set a trajectory of fearfulness in me. I choose not to go into detail about what was done to me. I will say that my innocence did not remain after that. I have a vivid memory of what was done and it has taken me years to process. The healing came much later in life. I was unaware that the actions that were taken against me were wrong. I was taken advantage of due to my age. One day my momma patted me on the bottom and I revealed to her that the thief patted me on my bottom, too.

"He did?" my mother inquired. "Well, what else did he do to you?" I began to very innocently tell her everything that had happened to me, not understanding how to explain it. I did the best I could.

Immediately, going into action, my mother marched up to the house and was stopped by our widowed neighbor. My poor mom was so devastated, she was angry and on a mission. She declared, "If he comes near my children again, I will kill him." She did what came instinctively, to protect her children. As a mother, I would have done the same.

Unfortunately, these types of incidents were not often reported to the authorities as they are today. There were no real ways of advocating for children who were abused, nor was there any counseling available for the victims. My abuse was kept silent because of fear. Fear of what the community would think of me or my parents, or perhaps I might have been fodder for gossip. Silence seems to be the golden ticket to surviving trauma or so some might have us think. Those people would tell you, "Let's just sweep this under the rug. Move along now, nothing to see here. Just don't say anything and just move on." This makes me incredibly angry. The thieves get away and the children and their families are left to deal with the aftermath of sexual abuse.

He was quickly removed from the area; I would assume by his sister, but I do not have the full details of how it happened. One day he was there and the next, he was gone, never to be seen again by me at least. His home was removed from the property. We did not stay in that area much longer after that. I was in my thirties when I found out from my mother that he had died in a house fire. I hate to admit it, but I was happy to hear that news. I thought it was justifiable punishment for what he did to me. This was also before I came to a place of healing.

Things began to surface for me when I reached adolescence. I still had not gotten any help to process or heal from my childhood trauma because, honestly, time had passed and I had no real idea that I was in need of help.

I was afraid to tell my story. I tried to reason with what happened to me, to make some sense of it. I do know I was sad and confused a lot. I was a constant bedwetter and had bladder issues. In my own way, I was not handling the stress of the event well. I did not feel seen or heard. I did not really comprehend the damage of these events until I was well into middle school age. I would think, I'm *crazy. I am making too much of this. It happened a long time ago, surely it cannot affect me now.* I was wrong and in deep denial.

Because I was introduced to sexual behavior at a young age, I became aware of arousal around age ten. I began to masturbate. I was trying to understand what this was all about. I had no understanding or teaching of sexuality at that time. I was devastated by masturbating because it felt like another dirty secret.

This coping mechanism led to a severely deflated sense of self-worth. I was convinced that I was a bad person because of what was taught about sexuality in my Christian upbringing. I sincerely believed that good girls remained virgins until marriage and that meant no masturbation or sexual arousal outside of marriage. I felt disgusting, and like a disappointment to God. I was so confused, and my body was having adverse reactions to my own curiosity – another effect the trauma had on me.

I went through my teen years still carrying around that shame and guilt of what had happened to me. I had a strong need to be loved and accepted by everyone because I did not know how to love myself. I remember having boys interested in me in my high school years. I wanted the attention, but when they got too close for my comfort, I would break it off. So I was labeled as a tease. In reality, I was terrified of intimacy because of the trauma I experienced and the lack of help I had in dealing with it.

By the time I had enrolled in college in the early '80s, I had figured out how to manage or keep the trauma at bay, or so I thought. But like dirt under the rug, it would surface from time to time. I was a clingy young adult, still looking for love and acceptance yet fearful to allow it to come close to me. Eventually though, I did find my person. I found love. I married the most caring and compassionate person. It took years of unpacking pain and fear for me to fully disclose everything to him. He was the first person that I pulled back the rug for and, to my surprise, he still loved me, even with the dirt underneath the rug. At this point, I still had not gotten any counseling or support around my longest held trauma.

Things began to resurface when we had our first child. When she turned four is when it hit me really hard. I was in a place of duality between mother and child. I was angry. I was confused. I became deeply depressed. I wanted to protect my child and make sure that what happened to me would never happen to her. I was living in two worlds. My daughter was safe and my inner child was crying out for help. Six years later we had another child. I was focused on being a mom and taking care of my daughters. All of my attention was funneled there. I loved it and it was a way of keeping me distracted. My own inner child was still crying out for help. She was screaming, "Can't you hear me? I am here. I need help. Please, somebody?!"

After both daughters grew up and ventured out on their own, my life became very quiet. I had no more distractions. Nothing to divert my attention. I began to take a really close look at myself. What had happened to me? I had not paid attention to my body and mind over these long years of neglect. I was depressed, riddled with anxiety, overweight and out of shape. There was a price I paid for sweeping the dirt under the rug and now it was time to begin to do something about it. I began by asking myself some tough questions and allowing myself to be honest with the answers.

I eventually realized that I was waiting for someone to rescue me when all along it was me who had to step in and recover the broken pieces of my life. Not anyone else! I began by healing my physical body. I started working out slowly. I began to love my body and pay attention to what it was needing. I went from barely being able to exercise to working out daily. I have also reconnected with my inner child by bike riding and roller-skating. These outdoor activities make me so happy and carefree. I am stronger and healthier and happier now. After focusing on the outer work, it was time to focus on the inner. I asked myself, "What's next?"

I began to feel strong enough physically to allow myself to go into my mind and delve a bit deeper. I enrolled in a health and life coaching school where I learned about habit and thought change. I found the courage to pull the rug all the way back and look at what was under there. Slowly I was able to sweep away the years of shame and guilt that had accumulated. I had no idea how much this would change my life. Having the courage to walk through this door continued to open more doors for me. Each step of my clarity journey continues to prove to be the best thing I could do for myself. When I began working with Allyson, she taught me about inner childhood work and about cognitive behavioral science. This very important work would be the missing piece to the puzzle that I was so desperately looking for.

It took me fifty-two years to find this missing piece. I finally was able to rescue little Michelle by using meditations and visualizing how to connect with my four-year-old self. This was also something that I learned from Allyson. She taught me how to go there. It still makes me proud when I think about it. I bent down and picked little Michelle up and carried her into the future with me. I let her know that she was safe now and no one would ever harm her again.

Little Michelle is now happily settled into the room of her dreams which faces the ocean on one side and the mountains on the other. She has all the toys and books she could ever imagine. We play together often and share stories and spend time together. This is all a part of inner childhood work. I am finally at a place in my healing where I can tell Little Michelle what she always needed to hear: you are safe. You are loved. You belong. The mind truly is a powerful thing!

You are safe now, my little one. I am here with you now. Together we will return to innocence, raise our voices, and tell the tale of survival and strength. We will use our voice to empower other children to rise up, tell their stories, and heal from their own trauma.

May you be brave as you begin your journey. You are not alone.

PATH TO YOUR POWER

How long has it been since you connected with your inner child? Was there something that happened to you that caused a disconnect? Meditation can be a great way to allow yourself to bridge the gap between the two of you.

If it is possible for you to locate a picture of yourself as a child, it can be a helpful visual as we begin to go into the meditation together. Lovingly and with compassion, look into their little eyes. Observe the face and body language. What are they doing? Allow your memories to take you back to that time.

If you could speak with them, what would you like to say? Allow yourself to let go of any guilt or fear you may have as you begin this meditation. Approach the child slowly and gently like you were trying to gain the trust of a small animal. Easy and gentle.

Begin by asking your inner child, "How can I support you? Is there something that you would like to share with me?" Allow yourself to be open and just listen to the inner child. When we approach conversations with curiosity and no judgment we allow space for open connection.

What beliefs does your inner child have about themselves and life in general? Do they need some encouragement? You can be the best person to offer that to them.

Invite them to come with you into where you are right now, into the future. What would be some of the things you would like to do together? Listen as your inner child shares with you and take note.

Is it more play? Perhaps adventure? How can you begin to tap into your inner child self? What did you like to do as a child? How long has it been since you tried it again? Would you be willing to give it a try?

What do you miss about being a child? Explore the answer by going to http://theclarityjourney.com/a-special-gift-for-you to access your free guided meditation. Use the password behindthepower22 to access the page.

Or scan the code below to access your free meditation.

ABOUT

Michelle Sullivan is a transformational life coach. She created The Clarity Journey coaching program. She is passionate about her energetic coaching methods and has a desire for all she works with to live with great clarity.

She is a sought-after speaker and teacher in addition to her one-on-one coaching. She is a Transformational Coaching Methods (TCM) Master Coach and TCM Transformational Coach. Her experience and training combine a powerful toolbox. Michelle is a true leader in her field. Her talks leave the audience encouraged to reach for what was once believed impossible.

She is a creative soul who loves to work with her hands. You can find her spinning on her spinning wheel, baking in her kitchen, or birding in the local forests of her home in Asheville, North Carolina.

Always stand in your POWER!

CHAPTER 5

THE SHOCK OF A LIFETIME

ERIN ARNETT

The day I got divorced started like any other day. The Florida sun was shining, and the palm trees were swaying in the breeze. The day consisted of standing before a judge and telling him I wanted to get divorced. Pretty uneventful.

That was before my world was turned upside down.

I had gotten married and had kids, and it all started to disintegrate. I won't say that this was an easy decision to make or a simple process, but there was not much to work out. We had worked out a custody arrangement, and that was that.

My sister had come for a visit and was waiting for me when I got home. After dinner, she gently pulled me aside and told me she needed to talk to me. It was then that she had one of the most life-changing conversations anyone has ever had with me.

As we walked around to the front of the house to get some privacy, I noticed how quiet she was. This was out of character for her. She had always been the outgoing one and the life of the party, so I was puzzled to say the least. My stomach was in knots and I couldn't figure out why. Then she started talking.

"I have to tell you something, but I don't know how to say it."

"What's going on?" I was immediately nervous and it showed.

After a few moments, she finally let it out, "He is a drug addict."

"Who's a drug addict?" I answered, very confused.

"Your ex-husband."

"Wait, what? How? Who? What?" I was so confused at this point. I couldn't figure out what she was talking about. She and her boyfriend had always been close friends with my ex and remained that way through the divorce, but I was completely clueless to this side of things.

"He's a drug addict," she repeated, and I still didn't comprehend what I was hearing.

"What kind of drugs? What are you talking about? You're talking crazy."

"All kinds, pot, cocaine, heroin."

Did she just say heroin?

"Yes, heroin," she answered. She must have seen the look on my face and knew what I was thinking.

After a few minutes, I finally found some words. "I know he's done some stuff, but I didn't think it was that bad. How do you know this?"

She avoided the question and tried to change the subject quickly, but there was no way that my sister would go through all of this if there were nothing more significant.

"You can't just say something like that and not tell me what is happening! So what is *really* going on, and how do you know this?" I was trying not to scream at her, but I was panicking.

She sat there for what felt like an eternity before she reluctantly divulged that she had gone down the same dark path that he had.

"You did what? Are you addicted to heroin, too?" I asked, obviously concerned and shocked.

"No," she replied. "I was, but I'm clean now." She further explained that getting clean was one of the hardest things she had ever done, but she had been clean for some time now.

Why was she telling me all of this now? Why not BEFORE I got divorced? Why did she wait until AFTER to say this to me?

My husband had gaslighted me, dismissed me, and told me I was crazy so many times that I was desensitized to it. It had just become part of everyday life. For the last couple of years, I lived in a numb state, drifting from one day to the next. I was never really sure which end was up, and this conversation with my sister only proved to muddy the waters even more.

She tried to explain that she didn't want to tell me at all because she didn't want to cause any problems or make anything worse for anyone, including herself. But, at the same time, she thought that I needed to know. She was concerned about how his addiction would affect her nieces, my children, and ultimately me.

I held onto this terrible secret for a while, contemplating if I wanted to confront him and going back and forth about it. Going on past experience, this would only result in more arguing and gaslighting. Eventually, though, I found the courage to confront him and, as expected, it did not go well. There was a lot of screaming and yelling, and I was threatened repeatedly that if I dared repeat any of this, I would "suffer the consequences."

Things only escalated from there. The ugly thing no one tells you about divorce is that the problems you had during the marriage don't magically disappear; in the worst cases, those issues get amplified. In my case, our poor communication during our marriage turned into dreadful communication after we divorced. We weren't able to talk without it turning into a screaming match.

After every argument, I would have the same thoughts. *Was I going to bring this up to him and demand an explanation? Or was I just going to cower down like all the other times? How bad was it going to get before I finally stood up for myself?*

We would meet halfway to pick up/drop off the kids in a fast-food parking lot. During one of these exchanges, he had gotten there before me. When I arrived, the kids were in the back seat of his car with all the windows rolled down, the engine turned off, and he was fast asleep in the front seat. I was horrified.

I got the kids out of the car; he never stirred. I put them in my car and went back and tried to wake him, but he wouldn't move.

I sat there for some time just watching him. He never moved a muscle. My brain was going crazy. I had gotten the kids out of his car, put them in mine, and just stood there for what felt like an eternity. *What if someone else had gotten the kids out of the car? We were in a busy parking lot. Anyone could have taken them. What if I had been even later getting there? How many other situations has he put them in where they were in danger?*

I mustered up all the courage I could find. I reached into the car and was finally able to wake him. I told him, "I'm taking the kids." I was so nervous to say this next part that I was shaking uncontrollably. "I'm not going to let you see the kids anymore." Then, still trembling, I turned on my heels and walked away.

He was quiet, but before I could get to my car, he started screaming and yelling at me at the top of his lungs. It was so loud and obscene that everyone started to turn and look at the scene he was causing. I was mortified but kept my head down, got in my car, and drove home. Luckily, the kids were none the wiser about what had happened that day or the amount of danger they could have been in.

As I sat there driving home with the kids in the car and, once again, trying not to have a complete breakdown, I was pondering how I had gotten to this point in my life. How had I let things get this bad? I had been carrying around so much guilt and shame about ending my marriage that I had not been able to see it. I was doing what I had been taught, the same things that my parents had done, and now I felt enormous guilt and shame. I was always taught to be a "good girl" and not make waves, but that was from a different time and era. I wanted out! I wanted to do things differently and didn't want to feel this way anymore.

This is where I decided I did not want to be stuck in my parents' story anymore. Up to this point, I had been too afraid to speak up or be heard, but not anymore. No matter what it took, I would never be able to forgive myself if something terrible happened to my kids because I didn't speak up.

This was the breaking point for me. I had a newfound sense of self. I felt empowered like I could rule the world. Well, most of the time anyway. Of course, there were still lots of ups and downs, but things finally felt different. Most importantly, I no longer involved myself in any more arguments. Instead, when the arguments and the threats started, I would calmly ask him to call me back once he had calmed down and then hung up the phone. I didn't want to suffer anymore, and I was done playing the victim. I was asserting myself, and it felt good!

Within a year, he was arrested when a concerned police officer found him fast asleep with drugs in the car. Then it became a cycle. He would be arrested, go to jail, rehab, get out of rehab, and proclaim that he was cured, only to be arrested again. This cycle continued for many years. I had been threatened repeatedly over the years and was constantly told that he would take the kids away from me to the point where I eventually believed it. But, once he was arrested, I found the courage to file for sole custody, so this could never happen again. Even with his drug convictions, it was tough to undo our original custody agreement, and I spent the next several years in court.

Through this time in my life, I was very numb. I can recall the events that occurred, but I was only present physically. I never felt like I had the option of experiencing life for myself, and now, I was trying to figure out how to juggle being a single mom raising two girls on my own and finding my way in life, all while fighting a custody battle with someone struggling with addiction.

Life as a single mother was a fight just to get from one day to the next. I was riddled with shame and guilt and struggled to reach out for the help I desperately needed. I didn't enjoy life during this time; everything seemed so difficult, and I felt it. I managed to get up every day, put a smile on my face, and pretend like everything was okay, at least on the outside. On the inside, I was falling apart a little more every day. If I couldn't be happy, I would try to make the kids happy, so I began to live my life around them. I made them my reason to get up every morning and keep going, a form of codependency that I can only now call out for what it was.

The struggle to overcome the mental and emotional abuse I had received over the years was long and daunting. I often wish he would have physically abused me because then there would be a bruise or a scar or something to prove how bad it had been for me and how much pain I went through. But unfortunately, all of my scars were emotional, and my demons were on the inside.

One night, while putting my kids to bed, my youngest turned to me and said she was happy that God had sent her to me even though I was sad and cried a lot. *Ouch!* Those words hit me like a ton of bricks. That simple statement from an innocent child broke my heart. I found myself in a heap on the floor of my bedroom for a long time that night, playing what she had said in my head repeatedly.

I had no idea I wasn't doing that good of a job hiding my sadness and bitterness from them. I thought I was doing a good job of shoving everything down and not showing how resentful I was that my life was being put on hold so I could deal with everyone else. I didn't realize how damaged I had become.

I didn't want to be like that anymore. It was not much of an existence, and I wanted to break the cycle. And most of all, I did not want to set this kind of example for my kids. I wanted them to grow up to be strong and independent women. I finally realized in order to do that, I must BE the example and become a strong and independent woman for myself. I had been the glue that held everyone together for far too long. I thought I had to be the strong one, the one that everyone depended on. It was time to stop feeling sorry for myself. It was time to do and be better. I wanted to 'feel' again. I didn't want to go from day to day as a zombie anymore.

I didn't know where to start or what to do. I had been like this for so long that I forgot what it felt like to feel. I began by *not feeling* sorry for myself anymore. It was robbing me of so much without me even realizing it. I started by taking better care of myself. I began eating better, getting more sleep, and getting outside more. No more staying up to the wee hours in the morning and then living off of coffee. I read plenty of books and tried things like yoga and meditation, but I struggled, so I settled on running. I didn't have much money, and the kids were still young, so I would run back and forth in front of the house while the kids slept. Slowly I began to smile more and feel like a human being again. The more my soul awakened the more I realized how asleep I had been for years. I had spent so much time under someone else's control that I had forgotten what it felt like to be me. I had allowed myself to believe that I was a horrible person and not worthy of anyone's love, especially my own. But not anymore; I was finally starting to undo all of the horrific suffering that I had gone through and become whole again.

It was definitely not all unicorns and rainbows. There were many ups and downs and lots of setbacks along the way. Over these years, I learned a lot of things. After being closed off and shoving down my feelings for so long, I had to learn to deal with not only the happy emotions, but the sad ones, too. All of these were new to me, and it took some time to get used to them. I learned that the bad feelings were just emotions that would only last for a few moments in time, so If I would just hang on for a little while, they would pass, and it would go back to not being so bad. I was finally able to build a better life, for myself and my kids—one where they felt supported and loved unconditionally, something I had never felt in my life.

My children are now grown and have families of their own. But unfortunately, they were never able to repair their relationship with their father. His addiction had gotten the best of him, and he eventually faded from our lives.

I realize now that going through all this pain has made me the strong and independent woman I am. I would have never been able to come this far without all the struggles. They forced me to rewire my brain, to set my own definitions in my life, and to embrace myself in my dark moments just as much as I do in my triumphant ones. The lessons lie not in the trauma but in the way we handle ourselves in the aftermath.

PATH TO YOUR POWER

Be kind to yourself. This is not easy; it takes time, energy, and effort. So be kind and forgiving to yourself.

Breathe. Take a moment several times a day to just breathe. Become present in the moment, clear your mind, and connect with your body. Breathe in, breathe out. This may seem difficult initially, but do this several times a day and watch the positive changes, like less anxiety. I know it seems silly that something as simple as breathing can ease your anxiety. But what have you got to lose? Give it a try, and you will be surprised at how much better you feel.

Give your habits an overhaul. Our habits are the things that we do automatically and define who we are. So, first, pay attention to the areas of your life that you are not happy with, figure out what bad habits helped create them, and trade those habits in for better ones. Next, try and figure out what behaviors will make the most significant positive changes in your life and turn them into habits. If you are struggling with this on your own, keep reading.

Pay for some help. Coaching makes you accountable and is the fastest way to make a significant impact. Find a coach who offers financing and reach out. Professional athletes don't just wake up one day and decide that they are amazing at whatever sport they play that day; they have coaches for their entire career. What makes you think you can do this yourself? You have spent the majority of your life already proving that you can't. Why wait?

Set honest goals. You're not going to run five miles tomorrow when you can't even run half a mile today. Start with small steps until you are confident and feel stronger. Discipline is a muscle and will not build itself overnight. If you bite off more than you can chew in the beginning, you'll get discouraged right away and quit. Set small goals *just* outside your comfort zone and work your way up from there.

Move. Your body will lead, and your mind will follow. When you get up and move, you have lots of energy and feel like you can take over the world. The mind and body together are more powerful together than either one by themselves. So get your blood flowing and eat something that excites you as well as nourishes your body.

ABOUT

Erin Arnett is an experienced Real Estate Appraiser in the Florida Keys, tech nerd, maker of silly t-shirts and anything with glitter, and a best-selling author.

She is a member of many organizations and enjoys donating her time and talents. This year she has stepped into the role of president of one of these organizations, a far cry from living a life terrified to ever speak up.

She is the mother of two grown daughters and an ever-expanding circle of friends. When she is not engaged in her many business ventures, she enjoys spending time on the water and with her crew watching football and thinking up brilliant new sayings for those t-shirts.

CHAPTER 6

A JOURNEY TO TRUTH

CHRISTINE N. COLE

It's one o' clock in the morning and my heart is pounding. *What is happening?* I can feel the blood rushing through my veins in every inch of my body. *Am I going to die from the morning after pill? Dear God, please help me! I don't want to die! I'm sorry, I'm sorry, I'm so so sorry. Please forgive me!* Tears stream down my face. It feels like this will never end. I can't sit still. I don't know what to do. I need help, but there is no one here who can help me.

My whole life I strived to do the right thing and to help people. I found joy in supporting others just to make their day a little easier. Through my good intentions I became a people pleaser and a caregiver. The wrong people recognized this and manipulated me, which led me to giving my power away to them. I didn't recognize the deceitfulness in these people until I was much older. I simply didn't know any better.

In my teen years and into adulthood I had spent so much of my energy trying to figure out what people wanted and expected of me. This failed because I wasn't being my true self. I stopped trusting myself and I felt lost, angry, sad, and alone. I felt a tremendous amount of desperation to be loved. This energy attracted partners who manipulated and took advantage of me.

At seventeen I lacked the social experiences most people my age seemed to have. I didn't smoke, drink, or do drugs because I believed, wrongfully so, that abstaining made me a good person. I intended to wait to have sex for when I was married.

The first experience was my junior year of high school. A senior named Mason showed interest in me. We were outside talking. I was cold. I had my back against his chest and he wrapped his arms around me. He attempted to grab my breasts. I quickly turned around, pushed him away, and ran inside.

Later that day Mason and his friend approached me. They were yelling at me saying he didn't assault me. Mason's friend threatened to hurt me if I told anyone. I was left feeling like I did something wrong and that there was something wrong with me.

At the age of eighteen I was getting my driver's license, buying my first car, and I worked for my father at his insurance agency. This is when I was introduced to Alex through a mutual acquaintance.

The first time Alex and I were alone in his house was the first time I was sexually assaulted. I made it clear to Alex I was not having intercourse with him. He tried convincing me to try oral sex. I didn't consent. We sat in his room listening to music when he started kissing me and undoing my pants. I told Alex to stop. I was nervous and uncomfortable and I tried to push him away. As Alex pulled my pants off I covered myself with my hands. He continued to force his head between my legs as I tried to stop him. I eventually and reluctantly gave in and let him have his way. I felt sick to my stomach, dirty, disgusting, and ashamed.

I ended things with Alex after this, but my self-worth had diminished so much while I was with him that when I met Owen he could clearly see I was easily manipulated by even the slightest bit of pressure. I would cave because I wanted to be loved. I settled and compromised myself for the sake of what I hoped was love.

I found myself in another vulnerable situation that I didn't see a way out of. Owen and I were alone in his bedroom. I thought I could trust him. Owen wanted to have oral sex and he promised he wouldn't penetrate me. He didn't keep that promise. I repeatedly said I didn't want to have intercourse. Things escalated when Owen decided to follow his own desires. I remember it being painful. I must have disassociated from the situation because all I remember was being rolled up in a ball sobbing when he finished. He went to the bathroom, and I went numb as I retreated to the darkest place within.

These traumas triggered a sex obsession. I couldn't get enough. I wanted to have sex every day. After Owen and I broke up sex became a tool I used to deal with my sadness and anger. It was a way to escape those deeply rooted feelings of disgust and despair I was struggling badly to ignore. I must confess, using sex the way I was made me feel degraded and dirty.

It was at this time I thought I met "the one." The more Carter and I talked I realized we wanted the same things. That was the beginning of me falling head over heels for him. I would have done anything for him and he knew it.

We were never officially dating, but we spent a lot of time together. I felt such a strong connection to him that I had convinced myself if I gave him what he wanted he would eventually see we were meant to be. My intuition told me he was destined for someone else, and I was heartbroken, but I still found myself hanging on. *What if I was wrong?*

One weekend Carter's friend Jaxon was visiting from his hometown. Jaxon was feeling low because his long-term girlfriend broke up with him. The three of us went to a bar to eat and have a drink. Carter asked me to kiss Jaxon. I did it. Then I kissed Carter. Things escalated quickly, and Carter suggested we go back to his apartment to have a threesome. I didn't want to and I was nervous, but I did because Carter asked me to and I was willing to do anything for him. I had no interest in Jaxon, and I can still remember pushing him away in some moments when he was getting too aggressive with me. It couldn't end soon enough and I was thankful when it did. I was humiliated, beat myself up, and buried the trauma deep inside. Jaxon went home and Carter was getting more distant after that horrible evening.

One night Carter called and asked me to go out for a drink. Unbeknownst to me this was going to be our last fling. He was getting back together with his ex-girlfriend. We went to the same bar where the bartender flirted with him mercilessly every time. It was one drink after another. I was so drunk I didn't know which end was up. We went back to his apartment and the clothes started coming off.

I sobered up quickly when we realized the condom broke. *Oh dear God, what did we do?* I was frantic. I ran in the bathroom to take a shower in my panicked state because I didn't know what else to do. *No, no, no, no, this can't be happening.* My whole body was shaking uncontrollably and my heart was pounding out of my chest. *Oh my God! What am I going to do?* I was more afraid of what my parents would think than anything else.

I made a doctor's appointment as soon as I could. I was nervous and praying to God that the test would be negative. As I sat at the edge of the exam table I explained to the doctor why I was there. I waited in nervous anticipation for the results. When the doctor came back into the room she said, "Well, looks like you're pregnant!" I was sobbing uncontrollably immediately. I was devastated and scared. *What am I going to do now?* The doctor's tone quickly changed and she offered me the abortion pill. I told her I needed to tell Carter first. She said

I had to take it within seventy-two hours of my positive test, and to come back if we decided we wanted the prescription.

I was acting calm, but I was extremely nervous. Carter asked if I wanted to go to dinner and I said we needed to talk first. We went for a long drive and I told him. Carter didn't have a visible reaction, but he offered to marry me. I told him no because he would end up resenting me and the baby later on. I told him about the pill and we decided it would be the right thing to do.

I went back to the doctor and she prescribed me the two doses. I stayed with Carter that night. It was one of the worst nights of my life. I thought I was going to die. I refused to take the second pill because of the physical reaction I had. I felt so much shame and guilt because I was supposed to be taking care of this precious life inside of me and I was not. It ate me up inside.

I was lost, scared, and completely alone. I didn't have anyone to support me through this process. I had to figure it out for myself. Every night I would sit in bed sobbing and praying to God for guidance. "I need help. I don't know what to do," I would mutter through my tears. *Please dear God, please help me.* I felt such darkness and despair. My insides were upside down. I had to hide this from my family. I thought they would be so angry and disappointed in me.

I debated having an abortion, but I couldn't bring myself to do it. A month later I got a yeast infection. Knowing I could miscarry if I used the prescription, I chose to take it anyway. At the end of the seven days I was in the worst pain I had ever felt in my life. The cramping was so bad it felt like someone was butchering me from the inside out. I could barely get up and shower. I couldn't stand up for very long. I miscarried. I was alone.

I fell into a deep depression. I had a desire to kill myself that grew stronger with each passing day. I slept all the time and barely got out of bed to eat. I had already graduated college so I didn't have any obligations. I didn't want to speak to or see anyone. No one called anyway. There was so much negative talk going through my head, I was convinced I was a monster and I deserved to die. I didn't bring anything valuable to the world. No one loved me and they manipulated and took advantage of me anyway. I wanted the pain to go away.

But God had other plans for me. Carter called me months later because he knew how angry I was at him and myself. He was being kind and acting concerned. Carter convinced me to go with him to a family wedding. It ended up being a three-week trip. The funny thing is he saved my life and had no idea.

The trip did not change what I was feeling or from being in the dark place that I was in, but it stopped me from ending my life. It stopped me because I didn't think his family should have to clean up my mess. In my mind it was not right to burden them.

My relationship with Carter changed me. I used to give people a chance until they gave me a reason not to. That was no longer true. I didn't trust anyone. I believed everyone was going to betray and harm me. I was angry and sad all the time. I threw myself into work and took all the overtime they were willing to give me.

I finally made the decision that I needed to focus on myself. I worked two jobs and little by little I gained distance from the relationship I had with Carter. I buried all of the trauma so deep inside I thought I moved on. Two years had passed when I finally stopped obsessing over him and went back to college, this time for graphic design. I was determined to live my best life. *If I can survive a miscarriage then I can survive anything.* That's what I told myself each day, and it gave me hope at the moment that I would find healing.

I had lost so much of myself over the years and had given all my power to the people in my life. In 2007 my life turned upside down. I was getting married, graduating college, moving to West Virginia from Massachusetts, and it was the beginning of twelve years of anxiety and panic attacks. I struggled to adjust. I didn't know I was experiencing culture shock alongside the anxiety and panic attacks.

The anxiety was severe enough that I became a shut-in. My healing journey began in massage school. I was encouraged to try acupuncture to ease my nervous system. It helped, but it was temporary. I was also introduced to an intuitive coach who gave me tools and meditations to support my healing. What I learned gave me some peace, but it was not the full solution. When we moved to Hawaii I was anxiety free for about two weeks, but I became overwhelmed again. I went to acupuncture, chiropractors, and still I was living in a constant state of fear and anxiety.

I was a complete mess. That's when I was introduced to my first intuitive coach. During my first session she explained to me that I couldn't discern between my energy and the energy coming in from the world around me. It was overwhelming. With my coach's guidance and taking her classes I gained tools to support me. Although, there was still something missing. I had a feeling there was more.

I was left with these tools that didn't seem to work for me anymore. I was still having severe episodes of anxiety and panic attacks. We eventually moved from Hawaii to Massachusetts and I felt completely out of place in my own life. All the spiritual and energetic work I had done felt like it had never happened.

After a great deal of loss and expansion over a three-year period I was introduced to Allyson Roberts. She teaches Personalized Science, the combination of brain work and spirituality. I didn't know it at the time, but I had finally found what I was missing with the other coaches. Combining cognitive behavioral therapy and spirituality was the magic combination for me.

By understanding the science of how the brain works I have been able to unearth the trauma of my past. I finally realized I was the only one who could rescue me. No one can do that for me. I became an observer. I am getting to know the real me through examining my thoughts, feelings, and beliefs. The spiritual work supports the brain work because it is a vulnerable process. I am healing childhood traumas that I didn't know existed. Getting to know my inner child has changed my world. I better understand myself through connecting to my younger self. The biggest takeaway is that healing is a lifelong endeavor. I am dedicated to continuing healing so I can bring healing to the world around me.

PATH TO YOUR POWER

Ask yourself this question: **Am I following my life or am I living the life people expect me to live?**

I have spent my life, until now, living the way I thought I was expected to. I looked to other people for direction and to make important decisions because I didn't feel capable. By doing this I gave my power away.

Do you give your power away?

This is how it has shown up in my life. I put everyone else before myself. Meaning I was not important enough to take care of. I became the caregiver of many in the sense I would sacrifice my own health, wellbeing, and what I wanted for the sake of others.

It has also shown up as codependency. Where all the emphasis was on other people and my mere existence was dependent on them. Does this sound familiar? I have sacrificed my integrity, worth, health, and so much more because I wanted to be loved by the world around me. What I didn't understand was if I loved myself first I would have everything I needed.

In my darkest hours I found painting. Painting created the space for me to just be. Painting gave me the freedom to create without the pressure of being perfect. Through the process I found peace and healing. You can pick any creative outlet to express yourself; it doesn't have to be painting.

Meditation is an easy way to connect to myself and God. I practice traditional guided meditation, but I find walking out in nature is when I get information from the divine. It also happens while I'm in the shower. I have all these "aha" moments that I write down or record in notes on my phone. This way I can refer back to the information when I need a reminder.

I have been introduced to inner child work by Allyson Roberts. The work has changed my life in ways I couldn't imagine. By communicating with different ages I am gaining awareness of traumas that I have buried and avoided. I am building meaningful relationships with myself and understanding why I think, feel, and believe what I do. I am able to heal and reveal more of my authentic self.

Journaling is another way to gain awareness of what I am thinking and feeling. Sitting with pen in hand, writing, reveals to me what is truth and what stories I've created. This is valuable because I discover where I need work and healing.

This work is not a solo endeavor. Having Allyson and the other Unapologetically Powerful students helps me to stay on track. Their love and support is key when I'm feeling stuck.

I pray you realize you are not alone. Healing is a journey that stretches over a lifetime. I encourage you to try my healing methods and to find support because you deserve to live your best life. Love you!

ABOUT

Christine N. Cole is best known for her work as an empathic communicator and painter. After being featured in Volume 1 of *Behind the Power*, she is also a best-selling author. Holding a Bachelor of Science in Communications and a Bachelor of Arts in Graphic Design from Salem State College, she is best known for her Soul Paintings. Combining her natural intuition along with her love for painting and the arts, Christine taps into loved ones who have crossed over and brings their message to life through art. Her paintings are unique, one-of-a-kind pieces that are changing the lives of people all over the world. Christine can also channel messages from our beloved pets who have crossed the rainbow bridge.

To schedule a session to receive your message from the Divine, contact Christine at soulpaintings72@gmail.com.

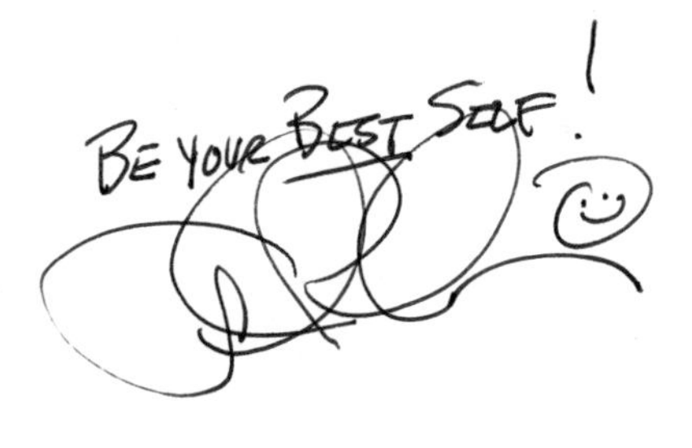

CHAPTER 7

A GRAIN OF SAND

JOHN ROBERT COLE

I was once told that even the smallest grain of sand, when dropped into a large pool of water, will make a ripple. While we may not notice it, that ripple has an impact. The fish may swim towards it, the plants may sway, and the slightest piece of earth may fall from the shoreline. That small grain of sand changes everything. Trauma is no different. It can be as small as a grain of sand yet create a ripple that lasts a lifetime. The only way to heal is to discover that grain of sand and address it, but it is not always easy. As I discovered, my trauma was well hidden, locked away in a memory I had no intention of recalling. It wasn't until I allowed myself to remember my past pain that I would begin to heal.

It all started when I came across an old black and white photograph of two boys sitting side by side. It was one I hadn't seen in quite some time. One of the boys–the one on the left–had a big smile on his face. That was me. I was two years old. The other boy, looking slightly sad and forlorn, was Charles. Charles was my half-brother, my father's son from his second wife. Along the top margin was a date printed in iconic Kodak sans serif. "November 1967," I whispered to no one. "This was taken the month before Charles' fourth birthday." For some reason, I felt a deep sadness. It then struck me that this fifty-four-year-old picture was the last one ever taken of the two of us together. Charles would disappear into the foster care system soon after and I would never see him again.

Those that remember him tell me he suffered from behavioral problems. I cannot speak to that. I cannot speak to my parents, either, since both have long-since passed. What I can say is that one day I had a brother and the next day I did not. I can also say that the unexpected loss of my brother created a fear so firmly rooted in my soul that it affected every aspect of my life for the next five decades. I was afraid that if my father could give up one son, he could give up the other, too, and I deeply hated him for that.

One warm Autumn afternoon when I was seven or eight, my father asked if I would like to play catch with a new football. I was both surprised and a bit apprehensive because I was neither a football fan nor a big kid. In fact, I was rather small for my age and preferred playing with my GI Joe or riding my bicycle. Still, he had asked me to play so I jumped at the opportunity.

Standing about twenty feet apart in a large patch of green grass he shouted, "Are you ready?"

"Yes!" I responded earnestly. The ball came flying in my direction.

I can still see that perfect spiral as the ball soared through the bright blue sky. I can feel the impact as that hard piece of pigskin hit me squarely in the chest. After catching my breath, I picked up the ball and tried to throw it back.

"No," he said firmly. "You need to put your fingers on the laces to throw it."

"I'm trying," I said, but I couldn't do it. My hands were too small. The ball wobbled and dropped short by more than half the distance between us.

Clearly irritated, he threw it back to me. This time I almost caught it, but it jammed my fingers and I started to cry.

That was the end of play. We would never pick up a football again.

I felt guilty for letting him down and ashamed for being so small. I was also terrified. While true it had been a few years since Charles went away, we never addressed it. In fact, my father rarely addressed any matters of the heart. Even the ubiquitous "I love you" was never stated, only implied. As a World War II combat veteran, he tended not to speak at all unless it was to yell. Like my father, I never spoke of my feelings. I didn't feel safe enough to share. Instead, I kept them to myself where they chewed away at my self-worth. I would often think that if I wasn't good enough to be my father's son, I was never going to be good enough for anyone else. My solution was to try harder and make everyone see that I was worthy.

But I kept failing.

I was the perpetual victim of the local bully on the school bus. I was too poor to have new clothes. My family didn't take summer vacations like my peers' families did. My grades were not good enough so I resorted to cheating on exams. At every turn, I failed. This made me angry. Very, very angry.

By the time I hit my teenage years, the damage was complete. I firmly believed that I was of little value, and it showed. I cared little for my appearance, took every criticism as a personal attack, and began to lose touch with myself. I often felt as if I were two people: the outward-facing angry me and the inner, remorseful, shameful me who just wanted it to stop. During my junior year of high school, I remember my best friend using his entire weight to keep me from punching my father in the face. I cannot recall what caused my outburst, but I remember how easily accessible my rage was and it scared me.

In 1984, less than a year after graduation, I eloped with a girl I had met during my driver's education class. I was so angry with my continued failures that I desperately needed a win. I thought marriage would rescue me and redeem me in some way.

It did not.

I disappointed my mom and further alienated my father. Worse yet, I made immediate enemies of my new in-laws. I still remember her mother literally blocking the door to their house as my wife gathered her things. "You will never be good enough to marry our daughter," she hissed.

Despite the guilt I felt, I was determined to prove everyone wrong.

We learned that we were pregnant within months of our marriage. Feeling an overwhelming fear of living on food stamps, I joined the United States Coast Guard – not out of patriotism or some deep-rooted humanitarian purpose, but out of necessity. Within the service, I found protection from myself as well as a decent salary. When I was in uniform, I had rank, privilege, and respect. I felt valued because I was able to follow the rules and complete the mission. Outside the service, on the other hand, life continued to erode.

My father passed away while I was underway on the Bering Sea on patrol. I was flown from Anchorage, Alaska to New York State to attend the funeral. I did not mourn his loss fully, and the consequence of that was losing what little emotional connection I had with my wife. We ended up separating. A few years later, I remarried. Again, I was expecting some sort of miraculous rescue and found nothing but frustration and anger. I felt as if I could never meet her expectations so I decided to leave after a mere two years.

I threw myself back into work because I was good enough for that. I quickly advanced in rank, earned multiple degrees, and was accepted as a member of the Officer Corps. Still, none of my achievements seemed to matter to me. The truth was, I never felt good enough because I truly believed I did not deserve anything good. I was never happy in love, marriage, or work because I had lost that connection to myself. For me, the most painful part was never retaining friendships from station to station; I simply did not deserve them. This led to deep feelings of loneliness and isolation which fueled my belief that I was built for rejection.

I married yet again in 2007, vowing that things would be different. I went in with a positive attitude intending to make it my life's purpose to make my new wife happy. Instead, we argued. I took everything personally and could not understand why she did not appreciate all the things I did for her. I convinced myself that our relationship would improve over time when, in truth, I felt as if another failure would destroy me. We lived in this toxic environment for more than a decade. This resulted in severe codependency that we are only now beginning to address as a couple and as individuals.

The final brick to my story was laid on February 13, 2020 when I was asked to say goodbye to the Coast Guard after more than thirty-five years of active-duty service. As my Captain put it when he broke the news that I would be mandatorily retired, "Compared to the others, you were simply outperformed."

Outperformed? I thought. *Isn't that another word for failed?*

The news hit me like a perfectly spiraling football I knew I couldn't catch.

As was tradition, I was offered a ceremony to reflect on my career. I walked to the podium, pulled out my notes, and proceeded to speak. I did not praise my superiors, joke with my colleagues, or tell stories to inspire. Instead, I projected my anger and utter disappointment for having failed the service and myself. In my mind, despite what others considered an illustrious career–the awards, the excellent evaluations, and the stellar work itself–I was clearly not good enough and it hurt.

For the next few weeks, all I could do was ruminate. Not only did I feel devalued, I felt as if I had sabotaged my speech and squandered an important milestone in my life. I was embarrassed and angry with myself so I turned to action. I accepted an uninspired job as a civil servant with the federal government at the very same location where I had just retired. I knew full well that I would despise it, but I aimed to prove the Coast Guard wrong and redeem myself.

I wasn't on the job for very long when I realized that I had made another huge mistake. This job wasn't going to prove anything to anyone. On the contrary, it was going to kill me. I had constant pain in my stomach, non-stop migraines, and an underlying anger that threatened to squeeze the very life out of me. I felt helpless. To quit would have meant another failure and I didn't think I could handle that.

Then things changed.

Late in 2020, I hired a cognitive behavioral expert. To be honest, I almost passed on the opportunity. At the time, spending "hard earned money" without receiving a tangible product in return was alien and scary. It took days of internal reflection to conclude that my reservations had nothing to do with the money but with my fear of admitting defeat. Once I accepted that, I knew I was ready to invest in me.

It was the best decision of my life.

My coach explained that I, like many of us, had experienced trauma as a child. Naturally, I scoffed at this. I said, "Sure, my childhood wasn't perfect, but it was far from traumatic. Nothing *that* bad ever happened to me." She then explained that trauma was not the sole proprietorship of those grieving or those who have suffered from violence, accidents, or natural disaster. By its very definition, trauma was *any* deeply distressing or disturbing experience. It could be large or small. More importantly, it was *personal.* In other words, trauma resulted from any event that changed a person's view about themselves or the world around them.

Understanding this made a world of difference.

I began to see that my persistent anger, fear, and codependency were all symptoms of a much deeper issue. Even my earliest memory of feeling unworthy–that of playing catch with my father–was a symptom. It wasn't until I found that photograph of Charles and I that everything made sense. My trauma–the one that had resulted in two ruined marriages and nearly a third, left me without friends, spawned continuous anger towards my father, and insidiously led me to doubt every decision I have ever made–stemmed from the loss of my brother to foster care. It changed my worldview.

Once I had this powerful breakthrough, I opened myself up to redefining the way I approached life. The first thing I did was relieve myself of that uninspired job. While the loss of income did affect my finances, it was not as severe as I had feared. Indeed, less money had the benefit of highlighting my intrinsic value as a *person.* I was finally able to fathom that money did not define me but rather I defined myself. I then started college to follow my passion for art. Next, I began to reframe my story, learning to tell it from a place of emotion and not of blame and anger. To do this, I remained patient with my younger self, befriending him, explaining as a father would to his son that his brother's departure had absolutely nothing to do with him. I tell my younger self he is safe and he is loved.

The true beauty of what I have discovered in this work is that my thoughts can control how I feel, and I do not have to live for the approval of others. These discoveries freed me from the prison I had built for myself. I now think what I want, when I want, and have the freedom to change my thoughts if they no longer serve me. I control me and me alone. This thought alone challenged my beliefs about codependency – and that is a very good thing.

Undoubtedly, the biggest impact for me was my path towards forgiveness; not of my father but of me. My father, while not perfect, lived within his own belief system. It was unfair for me to blame him for having his own thoughts. I, on the other hand, had a choice. Unknowingly or not, I was the one who adopted his belief system and I was the one who internalized all that fear and anger. Moreover, I was the one who allowed it to erode my self-worth and control my life. It served to reason that I was the only one who could forgive myself.

So I did.

I do not believe my grain of sand was the photograph. I believe it was the choice I made to heal despite the pain. My question to you is, are you ready? If so, make the decision. It is either yes or no.

PATH TO YOUR POWER

I will not pretend that I know your story nor will I pretend that I am an expert on abandonment. Truth be told, it was only recently that I discovered my decades of fear and anger resulted from my brother's removal from my life and not my father's behaviors, as I had previously thought. My "credentials," therefore, are based upon the idea that most, if not all, of us have, at one time or another, experienced something in our lives that changed everything. It may have been a moment, a series of moments, a thought, or a belief. It was something that changed our perception of ourselves or the world around us so deeply that it still haunts us today.

Let's try a quick experiment. Take a second to think of a time where you felt belittled, afraid, abused, or demeaned in some way. Try not to relive the experience but rather observe it. What do you see? How did that experience make you feel? What were you thinking? It's okay to be afraid or resist. That's normal. In fact, you will most likely tell yourself that it's too hard, that you can't, or that you don't know how. But here's the thing: if you were able to remember something that made you feel a certain way, if only for an instant, you have started your healing journey. It all starts when you acknowledge the pain.

Where you go from there, however, is a decision that only you can make.

As we both begin our journeys of healing and self-discovery, I would like to share some thoughts with you. If they resonate, please let me know. I would love to hear from you.

- **Question everything, even your own thoughts.** What you think and believe may not be true. In my case, I made up stories to fit the narrative that my father didn't love me when it really had nothing to do with him. I had to revisit my childhood as an adult to discover the real truth.
- **Take an interest in yourself and your story.** Remain curious about who you are. You are unique, special, and one of a kind. Ask yourself why you think like you do, why you feel what you feel, and notice any patterns. You may be surprised at what you find.
- **Be patient and compassionate towards yourself.** Healing is a marathon, not a sprint. It took me years to believe what I believe so it will take some time to change those beliefs.
- **Release all blame.** No matter what the circumstance, big or small, the way you reacted was entirely yours – even if

you didn't know any better or were forced into a particular response posture. The key is to acknowledge your decision and take personal ownership of your actions. Believe it or not, this is empowering!

- **Never stop digging.** What we believe tends to change over time based on the stories we tell ourselves to feel safe. Be the detective of your own life and never stop investigating.

ABOUT

John Robert Cole is a full-time artist who uses his talents to bring joy into the lives of others.

When not creating with paint, brush, cloth, or pyrography, he is writing. He has self-published more than 14 books including two travelogs, a graphic novel, and multiple genealogies.

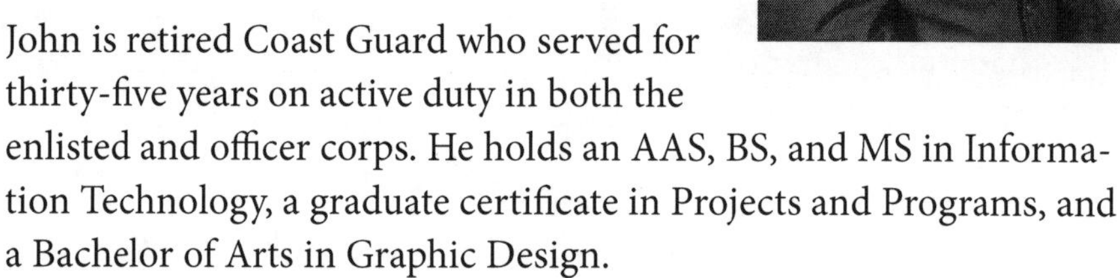

John is retired Coast Guard who served for thirty-five years on active duty in both the enlisted and officer corps. He holds an AAS, BS, and MS in Information Technology, a graduate certificate in Projects and Programs, and a Bachelor of Arts in Graphic Design.

You can connect with John at johncoleartist@gmail.com.

His other books can be found at: https://www.lulu.com/spotlight/celestialbay

You are enough!
Love, Donna

CHAPTER 8

CHAOS DOESN'T DEFINE ME

DONNA WALKER

If I think about that day that changed everything long enough I am right back in the first moment of chaos at home that I can remember. I vividly recall feeling on top of the world. This was the most wonderful day of my four-year-old life so far. Someone was noticing me and I felt connected with family. Something fun was happening!

My mother asked me to help her plant pretty little flowers. They were called pansies and had cute little faces on them. This was so exciting. I felt joy within to do this beautiful thing. The bright Texas sun was shining, and I felt like I was a part of everything.

Time passed quickly. I remember being so into the digging and setting the flowers in the dirt until the moment I was asked to go inside to get cigarettes and matches for my mother. I was a well-trained four-year-old; my job was to be perfect and to just do what I was told. This interrupted all the connection and fun I was experiencing, and I immaturely reacted. I felt more than angry, I was simply furious and ready to explode.

On the way back to the planting area I stopped at the garage. I had been told many times by adults not to light matches, but I knew how. I looked up and saw a shelf lined with newspaper. I decided to strike a match. I reached for the paper hanging over the shelf and it became an intimidating flame. I didn't see the fire spread, but I knew instinctively that it had.

I was starting to plant again on my own when my mother smelled something burning and saw the flames coming from the garage. The brightness of the flowers was no comparison to the blaze on the roof. The fire department came quickly, and so did the questions as to what started the fire. Denial of the deed when asked by anyone–my father, my mother, the fireman–was my first step into all the secrets I kept for so many years. My mother spoke to me in awful words I will never forget, "If you did this, you could have killed your baby sister who is sleeping in the house." I felt alone with my secret; the unspoken guilt haunted me. I felt stubborn and resolved to never tell anyone what I had done.

Things will be alright if I keep quiet and calm while doing what I am asked to do for others. I became the perfect rescuer – the one to make the morning coffee, the one to feed the animals, the one to wake up my father to go to work, the one who stepped in for anything that needed attention. I was always thinking, *Where is the next potential chaotic situation that I have to fix so everyone believes I am perfect?*

Another emotional, tumultuous situation started when I was seven and my sister was five years old.

A rescue from our teenage cousins was required after they violated us for a year. Sex at seven years old projected me into hiding shamefully and keeping more secrets. I felt dirty and unworthy. I remember sitting on the back steps listening to the older boys explain that my parents "do it" so it had to be acceptable; but we had to hide out and keep it secret.

We had an old garage which had been outfitted with blanket cushions for our sessions. We had to build tin forts later on because our parents were thinking we were up to something and told us not to go into the garage. The forts were small but visible from the kitchen where the adults were. I was chosen, since I was older than my sister, and I was talked into getting in the backseat of a car with one of them. That was the first time I was penetrated and it did not feel like anything that was explained to me. I decided nothing was worth that kind of pain and never did it again. I was old enough at seven and a half to start to understand that I was bad for doing this body part touching. I felt ashamed and unworthy. I was untruthful – I started disbelieving in myself. I started not liking myself. I started really hiding.

My ultimate solution to becoming a good, "clean" person was to ask my parents if I could join the Girl Scouts. My request was denied, "We have enough outdoor family and camping experiences already." In my opinion boating, fishing, and swimming were great activities, but watching my parents drink, fight, and fornicate was not so much fun.

Why do I feel alone? It seemed as though everyone in my family had learned the habit of self-sufficiency to a fault; whenever there was a problem we were trained to handle it alone, and the real staple of our family was never communicating. I wanted things to be perfect, and felt completely alone in that vision.

We were displaced from two houses because of house fires. (I didn't start those.)

The first fire was at night, and I remember standing outside across the street watching all the action and feeling alone, not knowing where my family was. This has remained a trigger story for me. I was challenged to find my family – my father was living with my brother in another city close by; my other brother was sleeping in a tent in the woods somewhere; my mother was job-hopping or missing and I would have to go to the police station to find her; my sister was married but moved around so often that it was difficult to know where she was.

We stayed in rental houses in Austin mending broken pieces attached to an already

broken existence. The first fire caused us to lose our clothing from fire, smoke, and water damage so we had to borrow apparel from friends. Both of these house fires required us to move for a few months before returning to our renovated homes.

When I was seventeen I responded to another emotional chaotic fire between my parents. I saw what I thought was the perfect moment to step in and a screaming match ensued. I let my opinion be known and ended up with a face slap from my mother. She told me she knew my father and I were having sex, and if I didn't like the way things were, I could just get out. I was so confused and had no way of proving to her that I, of course, wasn't sleeping with my father. She was convinced I was.

I stayed away from home as much as I could. I worked two summers in North Carolina at a Christian Retreat Center until I finished high school and went to college in Alabama earning a Bachelor of Arts degree, a Bachelor of Science, and a Master of Science degree – with no family member attending any of the graduations. I felt disconnected from my home in Texas and from my siblings. My sister professed that I had abandoned her and my brothers. When I left home for college, this became another guilt factor in my story.

Alcoholic families hide many secrets and we had our share. There was physical and psychological abuse. Instability and constant chaotic behavior produced personalities of shame and guilt. The insidious results of this upbringing had lasting consequences. My sister's anger and stubborn idea that she could make a horse respond got her thrown off, causing her to become a paraplegic, unable to walk for the rest of her life. One brother died of diabetic complications and the youngest brother is serving a three-life sentence in the Texas prison system. My family saw hospitalizations, incarcerations, unwise life choices, and perpetual fear of trusting others.

Chaos struck again when I became pregnant in my senior year of college. My fiancé was in the military serving in Vietnam. I was angry at him for leaving school and joining the Army. It did not seem like a practical life choice to give up on his education at this time – after all, we were engaged. The college classmate with whom I had an affair was not a stable husband choice. I knew just the professor who helped pregnant girls in trouble at the school. My psychology professor had a friend in Mexico who might want to adopt my baby. I went across the border to meet him by myself, trusting a positive outcome from the encounter, but eventually I came back home, still pregnant and without adoptive parents.

Upon returning, it was so easy for me to be bonded with my psychology professor, the one who attempted to rescue me, that when he asked me to live with him and his established family–two wives and five children–I agreed. I lived thirteen years with this family first in Alabama, then in Georgia. The idea of being part of family and belonging to a group of stable, intelligent, and successful individuals seemed like the best option for me.

I didn't look beneath the surface far enough to take assessment of the real situation being not what I first imagined. I had been told that this could be a cult – no way would I believe that.

I was blinded by having found my family. I was not alone.

My baby was not accepted into the "family." I put her up for adoption and went to her birthday parties with the wonderful adoptive family for her first eight birthdays.

I still tried to attain a perfect lifestyle and be perfect by my own arbitrary definitions and

standards. Deep down, though, I felt like I needed rescuing. The traumatic implosion of living in my chosen "perfect" family became a series of emotional torments, all of which stemmed from living with this narcissistic sociopath in a non-traditional situation. After I finally told him I was not happy with him seeking additional women outside of our circle, he responded with a cold, "Is that all?" And went on to tell me that was my only chance to share that and to never bring it up again. I felt a fire burning in me again.

The turmoil within could only be satisfied by me becoming unfaithful in my attempts to soothe my jealous soul. I became pregnant again on a trip out of the country and since I was frightened by the anger this would certainly incite from the one who wanted to hear no more from me, I had an abortion. I made the decision to stay in the "family" with yet another secret. My attempts at achieving the perfection I craved proved disastrous to my self-worth and sanity. I did eventually leave the narcissist to his selfish ways, but I continued making poor choices in my scattered attempt to figure my life out.

I was looking for the path that would lead me to be perfect: the best educator, the best wife, the best painter, the best gardener, the best at anything I put my mind to. Whenever I did achieve anything, I felt an overwhelming sense of imposter syndrome.

When I was nominated teacher of the year, I was convinced there must be a more perfect candidate. Surely I was not the best option

– there had to be some kind of mistake. After years of longing for validation and recognition, I rejected it. At my lowest points, I idealized death and made suicide attempts.

I could be the number one rescuer for everyone except myself. I still craved family, love, and support. I became clingy to anyone who even looked like someone seeking help, especially if it involved a family or ministry. I loved contributing to systems that worked. It helped me ignore what wasn't working internally. Where had all of my power gone?

I was so comfortable in my chaotic comfort zone. The more frenzied the situation, the more comfortable I was because I had something to fix. Yet, I was so uncomfortable with myself. I knew what I liked to do, but not who I was supposed to be. My insides were a burning mass of undeveloped personal respect. I became very good at hiding my insecurities. Nothing was more pressing than my desire to be perfect. I agonized over details that didn't matter and was a classic over thinker. I was perfectly miserable. My goal became to find the answer to my search.

Then I met the Recovery Queen, as I call her, Allyson Roberts. I am now finding extreme healing; progressing mentally, physically, and spiritually. Allyson invested her time rewiring me to love myself, to trust and receive support from others, to change my core beliefs and live a vision to accomplish my intended purpose in life. I am learning to not be tolerant of abuse, pain, manipulation, and chaos. There is a higher ground far away from malevolent thoughts caused by years of not feeling loved, appreciated, and supported. Allyson captures my attention with "the look." It says to me: "Trust my smile that is bursting to tell you, there are tools, there is love and support. You are worthy because you breathe." My search to find the power in me is now so rewarding. Use the tools, establish the boundaries, be present with awareness, observe, be creative, and most importantly, trust the process.

Life has led me to many places and I am still working on figuring out my journey. I am accepting the courage it takes to know and love who I am created to be and to understand my true authentic self. I may not be perfect, but I am enough. I am on a mission to complete my life's purpose enthusiastically and joyfully – learning to connect my humanity with the spiritual life inside that craves to be a whole, well-balanced child of God.

I start each day now with positive agreements. I am aware of my boundaries and I make good choices. I am the source of my time and use my energy to fulfill a new purpose:

to exhibit the confidence of the power in me. I love organizing my life and enjoy

being me and sharing with others important experiences that let them see the empowerment of their being. Healing is possible; you just have to see the power within.

PATH TO YOUR POWER

My desire is for you to appreciate yourself, love yourself, and find the expression to stabilize how you work and live passionately in your purpose. Be you – a confident person of power from the inside out.

The Power:

Finding the hope in your humanity is the acceptance of who you really are. Use your power to release the feelings of needing to be perfect and to control everything. Just being you, the real authentic you, is what is important in life to raise your self-worth. You are someone already loved and appreciated. It is important to love yourself and appreciate your value in the world.

The Power in You:

Be willing to change your narrative. Examine the stories you tell yourself and rewrite them. There is no need to live criticizing yourself and blaming others for your unhappiness. Be willing to receive the good that is there just for you simply because you exist.

The Power in Your Purpose:

Connect to a spirituality that includes your whole person and makes you joyful for being alive. Your power is in the acknowledgement of your purpose, changing every season and flexing with the nature of the moment. As you are seen and heard you will draw love and abundance to your sound mind.

The Power in Healing:

Be active in finding the moments in your life where emotional wounds went unhealed. Honor those moments. Heal your mind – thinking, feeling, and believing. Trust your new thoughts.

The Power Over Fear:

Turn around and see the dreams ahead of you. No more sulking or blaming. Face your new day with power and strength over insecurities; feel a new feeling. Believe that you are moving away from torture, pain, and manipulation. You are loved; you are safe.

The Power to Walk Secure:

The time is now. Find peace and stability in the power within you. Allow yourself to be comforted by connection with your support people. Walk without the pressure of keeping perfect action ready for everyone. You deserve peace and calm after the chaos – be aware that you can breathe fresh healthy love from boundaries you now create from new perspectives; honor a new mindset with new values.

Establish responsibility for your own life. Call on the force within you to show you there's a real power – the power in you. Retrieve a belief in you and watch your life transform.

ABOUT

Donna Walker is a retired Foreign Language teacher certified in French and Gifted Education. Her degrees are a Bachelor of Arts in French; a Bachelor of Science in Secondary Education; and a Master of Science in Education. Donna taught in the Fulton County School System for forty years.

Her leisure time is spent editing newsletters and playing outside with her two dogs, Abby and Tiana. Donna has entries in Who's Who of American Women and has published poetry and made contributions in multiple book series. She has spoken in National Teacher conferences on the teaching techniques of Joseph Renzuli for the gifted child.

CHAPTER 9

REDEFINING MY "NORMAL"

BLAIR SHIVER

I was around nine years old and standing in the front hallway of our one-hundred-and-fifty-year-old farmhouse. My mom was seething, and I was frozen, confused, and afraid. My dad was either still sleeping or off in the woods hunting, I can't remember which. It was Christmas morning, and I was eager to open presents and have our special breakfast casserole.

Christmases in our house were always the same, and full of tradition. After we attended Christmas Eve service at our small Episcopal Church, I would come home and be off to bed while Mama played Santa and put together the savory casserole of eggs, sausage, cheese, and bread that would sit overnight. On Christmas morning, Mama would break out my grandmother's antique Juice-O-Matic, and we'd squeeze fresh juice from the oranges stuffed into our stockings while the casserole baked.

But this year was going to be different; that's why I remember it so well. That was the year Christmas kind of lost its magic for me… because I saw something in my mom I'd never seen before. She was generally a pretty calm and level-headed person, but on that day, she was a woman who had reached the end of her rope. To this day, I have no idea why my mother snapped, but she decided to tell me some pretty horrific things about my family, including that my grandfather, my dad's dad, had taken his own life right before I was born. She followed that with telling me that my father had been abused by Catholic priests when he was a boy. I felt overwhelmed and confused. I was far too young to comprehend anything she was telling me.

Only now that I'm a mother can I begin to fathom the level of processing my mom was probably going through on her own, and that she was probably triggered that day by all of the traditions and expected normalcy when there was a lot happening beneath the surface and not being dealt with. My mother had no access to therapy; that wasn't a widely accepted or practiced part of mental healthcare when all of this happened, and I am positive she had no way of knowing how her dealing with this would impact me. How could she have known?

It's amazing to me how we subconsciously repeat so many of our parents' behavioral patterns. I knew my mom was considered a "later in life" mother for the times when she gave birth to me at thirty-three years old, and I was never in a rush to have children. I didn't grow up with tons of baby dolls, dreaming of the day when I'd have a family of my own. It just didn't seem to be a hugely significant part of my core being.

My parents met in 1968 at the University of Georgia. Women were not permitted at that time to even walk across campus wearing shorts; she had to wear a raincoat over her bare legs even on a bright, sunny day. By the time she graduated in 1970, hot pants and halter tops were in style and widely accepted on campus. It was a time of rapid and pretty drastic change.

I grew up in a small rural town. My father practiced law, and my mother stepped happily into her role of doting and supportive wife. They joined local civic groups, attended church, and hosted epic tailgating parties on Saturdays when the Bulldogs were playing football.

My parents argued most often about finances, and as I began to unpack my childhood memories, I realized there was a lot of insecurity around money. My father questioned every cash withdrawal my mother made and balanced their checkbook obsessively, scrutinizing every purchase from grocery bills, to car maintenance, and swimming pool repairs. Yet, he would frequently misplace his own checkbook or make purchases that my mother never questioned. There simply were not healthy conversations around financial health and security, and my journey into early adulthood provided many instances for him to try to exert control over me with money.

I'm not sure when my mom began putting her plans in place to separate from my father, but she discussed it with me as soon as she had viable options on the table. She said it had always been her dream to live in a coastal community, so she accepted a position, moved five hours away, and prayed I would join her. I did for about a year, but I longed for my friends and the familiarity of the only community I'd ever known. I opted to return to my small hometown of Elberton to attend high school and chose to live with my father.

Between maintaining my grades, working a part-time job, and cooking dinner most nights (he often grumbled about my frequent use of Hamburger Helper), the normal roles of parent and teenager dynamic, especially that of a father and daughter, were starkly different than most of my friends' families.

My parents decided that perhaps some counseling might help me process the divorce and subsequent moves back and forth between my parents' homes. It felt good to process some of the pain I'd been stuffing down, hiding behind my facade of strength and teenage indifference. *Why would my mom want to leave me?* Even though she openly discussed it with me, I simply assumed she never would leave; that she would suck it up and make the best of a bad situation. *Why would my dad, with his own unhealed childhood wounds and loneliness after divorce, want to be strapped with raising a teenager alone?*

Within the first few days of my freshman year at college, I again did what was expected of me; my parents were members of a sorority and fraternity, and so I took part in sorority rush. However, shortly after pledging, I opted to exert some authority over my own life and, in my first major act of rebellion, chose to withdraw from sorority life. However, because I was deviating from my father's plan for what he felt my life should look like, he threatened to cut me off financially. We finally reached an agreement: I would enjoy my freshman year of college, but if I was not going to join a sorority, I would need to find a job.

After I graduated, he graciously helped me purchase my first home. It was beautiful, the model unit in a new construction project in a small coastal town in the Florida panhandle where I'd accepted a job after interviewing for an upstart travel magazine. Because he helped me move into this place, he began to feel entitled to come and go as he pleased. When I came home from work one afternoon he was watching television in my living room, oblivious as to why I might be upset about this. That was the moment I began to understand his lack of comprehension for normal parental boundaries.

Fear of failure has been a self-imposed limitation to keep me playing small.

We create stories about ourselves. Maybe you want to be a sideline reporter for ESPN, but don't think you're pretty enough for television, so you choose to become a writer behind the camera. Or maybe you want to be a psychologist, but you tell yourself building a practice is too hard and graduate school means student loan debt, so you settle for what's safe. You play small and ignore what lights you up and sparks your flame; that is the flame that will make your dreams come true, but you simply won't light the match.

This kind of fear is not rational. It's a trauma response that is meant to keep you in your comfort zone, away from growth and healing. You have to push this fear away; dump it in the garbage. It's like processed sugar. You can live without it.

I worked for a couple of years in the booming real estate market in New York City before a working vacation in the Florida Keys turned the page to my next chapter.

Michael was the cute, long-haired bartender serving cocktails and laughs in my cousin's restaurant. He made me laugh and offered a soft balance to my hard edges. Quite the opposite of my parents' prescribed path to family and marital bliss, we took life as it came and enjoyed the laid-back island lifestyle for a bit. We eventually set about the tasks of growing up, getting married, purchasing a home, and building a life together, but we didn't have the easiest time starting a family.

Though we didn't endure the hardships or financial challenges with in vitro fertilization and adoption, it took us a couple of years to finally conceive. I decided we would be the couple who rescued and cared for dogs instead of children, and when I was set on that path, we finally got pregnant. I secretly doubted my ability to be a mother, to nurture and love and care for someone other than myself or a partner. Occasionally when I couldn't sleep during my pregnancy I would toss and turn and question my preparedness for this life I was bringing into the world. *Will I love my baby enough? Will I make the same mistakes my parents made? Will my wounds scar my child as my parents' wounds had scarred me?*

Almost six years into my journey as a mother, I'm learning there's no greater teacher in patience and personal development. At our first sonogram, our doctor told us we were having a little girl, and for reasons I'm only now beginning to understand, I cried when I called my mom and told her the news. "Girls are emotional and dramatic… raising a boy would be so much easier!" I wailed into the phone and was met with her calming words of reassurance that I needed more than I realized.

I remember explaining to one of the nurses in the hospital shortly after Amelia was born that I wanted to breastfeed because it would be easier. She laughed as she recalled her four-year-old daughter slamming the door to her bedroom just a few days prior. "There's nothing easy about being a mom," she assured me.

Now I realize that God sent my daughter to me as part of my own healing journey. While, just like anyone, girls can be dramatic and emotional, they are also passionate, strong, fierce, determined, resilient, kind, caring, and gentle.

My daughter is also the reason after years of therapy, medications, and my own mental health struggles, I've embarked on this journey of breaking those familial patterns of yelling and reactionary anger. I am not teaching my daughter to be hung up on money the way my dad was, nor to settle into a life just because she thinks she has to. Although I was not the mom who read every parenting book ever written, I leaned hard on friends and family for advice. I was told by many people that there was no manual to parenting, that it's a try-as-you-go kind of thing. All I knew going into it was that I wanted to be different for my daughter.

Amelia was about a month old when I packed her up and took her out of the house to a baby shower by myself. The expectant mother was asking me about nursing and my birthing story, and I remember waving over another new mom. "The first month is the hardest," she told us. "If you can get through that, the rest is a breeze." She also reminded us that nursing is like a full-time job, and with those words, I allowed myself some grace. My child was healthy. I was doing okay.

In the post-Covid era of social media stories, influencers, and information overload, it's so tempting to fall victim to the trap of comparison…you know, that old thief of joy? *Do I spend enough time with her? Am I a helicopter parent? Are my anxieties and fears going to become her anxieties and fears? Did I break her little spirit when I raised my voice at her or lost my cool? Can I instill in her the confidence she needs to make choices in her own best interest and not for the approval of others?*

I've embarked on this journey to heal my own childhood wounds so my daughter isn't littered with quite so much of the same junk from her parents that I received from mine. We talk about money, but at an age-appropriate level for her understanding. Instead of exerting control through manipulation and financial management, we talk about highlights and lowlights and things for which we're grateful. I place zero expectations on her when it comes to defining her life. I teach her love, generosity, gratitude, and respect. I try to make her feel safe at all times so she knows she can always come to me. That is the most important role as a parent. Healing my childhood wounds is the most important thing I can do to be a better parent for Amelia. I am teaching her to define her own happiness by actively defining mine and letting her see the benefits of living authentically, with a strong foundation and boundaries.

When I screw up, I try to be honest with her. I do the thing my parents never did with me: I apologize. I explain my actions so she understands much sooner than I did that her parents are simply human, not perfect beings, and that she is loved above all else. I find myself speaking to her in a way that heals my inner child as well.

I hope when she hears me say, "Mommy shouldn't have raised her voice. If it scared you, I'm sorry. Mommies make mistakes, and my mistakes–of which there have been many and there will certainly be plenty in the future–don't define me," that she understands the unconditional love I have for her.

If I can succeed in breaking the generational expectations and traumas that were placed on me as a kid, and raise my child in a less toxic, more loving, and nurturing environment, then I will have completed one of the most important steps on this healing journey. I am working every single day, through the highs and lows, to make sure I succeed.

When radical personal responsibility is taken for healing old trauma wounds, and when there is acceptance of what your role is in this beautiful universe, there are learning opportunities in each moment and in every relationship. When there is a willingness to learn, no matter the situation, that is when true healing and happiness can be reached.

I am proud of my progress, but I know there is so much more work to do. I still have to rewrite parts of my story, but I am no longer afraid. I am no longer operating from a place of wanting approval. I am finally ready to do this for ME.

I owe it to myself!

Everything you've ever wanted is on the other side of fear.
– George Addair

PATH TO YOUR POWER

Here are three effective ways to elevate emotional I.Q. with children:

Active Listening. Listen to understand...not respond. As a recovering people pleaser, I've had forty years of training on saying what people want to hear. As a result, I've lost my voice as part of my childhood conditioning and have subsequently felt that I had to yell to make my voice heard.

Both personally and professionally, your family, friends, and colleagues deserve to know you're holding safe space for them without the desire to manipulate the outcome.

Practice active listening for three-to-five minutes each day. Jot down some new information that you learned as a result.

Internal Regulation. Learn how to regulate internally in order to succeed externally. You cannot nag, berate, belittle, or shame anyone into changing their behavior to suit your needs and desires.

What is a recurring thought you have on a regular basis that you wish you could change?

Setting Healthy Boundaries. No is a full sentence. Until you uncover and proclaim out loud to the world what you want and need, you will remain in a state of anger and/or frustration that other people are not saying, providing, and supporting in a way that meets your ridiculously impossible standards. With the exception of a few, most people are not mind readers.

What pattern do you keep repeating that you desire to change? What could you do differently?

ABOUT

Blair Shiver-Nealis is still trying to figure out what she wants to be when she grows up. In the meantime, she's grateful to be mom to a spunky little firecracker of a human being; partner in life and business with her husband as owners of a fabulous Florida Keys health food cafe and market; and cheerleader for people across the country regaining control of their own personal physical and mental health.

A University of Georgia graduate with a BA in Journalism, Blair enjoys exploring the beautiful waters of her island home as well as running and working out with friends.

All the Best! Jennifer Etzwiler

CHAPTER 10

BREAKING EXPECTATIONS

JENNIFER ETZWILER

My father died on February 19, 2018. That also happens to be my mother's birthday. Mom and I were planning to go out for manicures and pedicures. My stepmother, who is surprisingly good friends with my mom, had texted my mom earlier to say that she was taking my dad to the hospital because she thought he was dehydrated from the chemotherapy for esophageal cancer. My mom and I were getting ready to leave the house.

> "Have you heard anything from Janine? It's been a while. Doesn't she usually check in by now?" I was more curious than worried. This was not the first time my dad had been in the hospital.
>
> "You're right. I'll text her." Mom seemed a little concerned.
>
> Less than five minutes later, the phone rang. Mom answered, "Oh, okay. I'm sorry. I'll talk to you later."
>
> She turned to me as she hung up, "Your dad died in the emergency room."

I don't remember feeling anything. I wasn't surprised, or sad, or anything. It just was.

"Oh..." I was frozen for a moment. "Do you still want to go for mani-pedis?"

"I don't know. I'm not sure that's really appropriate."

I laughed suddenly, surprising myself. "I just got a picture of Dad coming with us in spirit, sitting in the spa chair, soaking his feet," I smiled at the thought, while my mother looked appalled.

We shared a bittersweet laugh, then she said, "Let's just go another day."

I never really thought of my dad as a superhero until just before he died. One day, I had this realization. *My gosh, if my dad wasn't around, I was going to have to be an adult! Oh, crap! I won't be able to go to him for help when I can't solve a problem. I was going to have to figure it out on my own.* I didn't go to my dad for a lot of my problems, but when I did go to him for help, it was because I wasn't able to figure it out, and no one else could help me either. Dad always came up with something.

When I was a teenager, I really wanted to go to cosmetology school to be a hairdresser. It was the mid-80s and big, new wave hair was the thing. My favorite place was the hip beauty school not far from my home. I could have hung out there and watched them do hair all day long.

It was expected that I would go to college. It wasn't just my family that expected it, but everyone around me. Every teacher, every family member, every adult would tell me, "You *must* go to college to get a good job so you can earn more money and have a better life."

It took a while to work up the courage to tell my dad I wanted to do hair. He had control of the college fund, so he needed to be on board. When I finally told him what I wanted to do, he said, "Well…if that's what you *REALLY* want to do…but I think you are too smart for that." There was disappointment and disdain all over his face.

I so internalized the second part of that statement that it was like the first part hadn't been said at all. It was what I really wanted to do, but I wasn't willing to feel like my dad respected me less because smart people went to college. I wasn't willing to fight an uphill battle for the next ten years because he thought I was too smart for a job that didn't require a four-year degree. I wasn't willing to risk the possibility that my dad might love me less.

My grandfather never went past the eighth grade. I heard so many times how one of the things my dad's father was proudest of was that all of his grandchildren went to college. Even though I went, I'm the only one of eleven grandchildren to not complete a degree. I've compared myself for years to the rest of those incredibly smart grandchildren and felt like I was a disappointment. I have carried a lot of shame and guilt throughout my life because of it.

I've been told since elementary school how important good grades were for my future. My fifth-grade teacher used to give us a lot of homework to prepare us so we would do well in middle school, so we'd be prepared and do well in high school, where we needed good grades to get into a good college. Then we could get a good job and make good money. *Phew, that's a lot for an eleven-year-old!* I was told, by just about every teacher that I ever had, and every adult that I encountered, that I could be anything I wanted to be when I grew up *— as long as it involved going to college.*

The rules were so clear to me in high school. I understood how things worked and the system in place was very clear to me. Teachers communicated, I was seen and heard by the administrators and students. I aced classes without an issue.

College wasn't like that. When I went to the advisors, 90% of the time I was assigned someone who was only there for the quarter, and it seemed to me that the communication was severely lacking when the advisors rotated. They never sounded very sure of themselves. I didn't seem to believe the advice they gave me. There wasn't continuity and the system in place confused me. Each department that I needed to interact with, whether it was the registrar's office, student affairs, or financial aid, seemed to be operating independently of one another and not communicating whatsoever. I was left feeling like just a number in the system there. No one would fully explain things to me, and when I would ask questions I was made to feel like a bother; everyone else seemed to be grasping the whole concept of college and I felt completely out of place. I didn't understand. I felt lost. Nothing made sense. It was like trying to work a jigsaw puzzle, but I couldn't find pieces that fit together.

I know, now, that deep down, I didn't want to be in college. My pattern was that when things got hard, I quit. There was so much expectation to go to college that quitting altogether didn't feel like an option. I would quit each class as it got hard, feel like a failure, register for more classes, feel out of place, drop out again, and the cycle continued.

I had this internal story that in order to be good enough, I needed to get As in school. The *occasional* B eventually became acceptable in my mind. My parents paid me for As in middle and high school. I got paid double if I got straight As. Scoring anything below a B+ was just as scary as a flunking grade. My self-worth was tied up in my good grades.

I procrastinated a lot in college. The procrastination would get me far enough behind that either it was more work than I was willing to put in to get an A, or I was just too far behind to get there at all. Then I would drop the class. If the class was hard and the material didn't come easily to me, it all happened much faster.

I spent ten years taking classes, but I didn't manage to finish a two-year degree or even a certificate because I kept quitting. It was depressing. I told myself over and over that I *did* want to be there, and I couldn't figure out why it was so hard, but telling myself that I wanted to be there wasn't enough.

I can still see the registrar's office in my mind whenever I had to walk through the doors to sign up or drop out of classes. I felt numb every time. If I was there to sign up for classes, I was numb but hopeful that this time I might follow through and finish all my classes for the quarter. If I was dropping classes, I was numb and ashamed that I was there to drop classes *again*. I can still remember the woman who worked there most often when I came in. She never seemed to judge me, but I harshly judged myself.

I felt like a waste. I wasted so much time going to college. I wasted a chunk of my life going to college. I wasted a lot of money while I was in college and felt even more guilt over most of that money being my father's. I wasted energy going to college. The energetic and emotional costs of continuously doing something I didn't want to be doing was very high. It weighed on me then. It still weighs on me now.

Even the money that I asked for to help pay my living expenses while I went to school felt like it had been wasted. If I had been working full-time, I could have taken care of myself financially. I enjoyed my job far more than I liked my classes.

If something didn't come easy to me, I didn't do it. If circumstances weren't perfect, I would skip it. When things got hard, I quit. I have learned that not understanding the larger picture or process is a big trigger for me. There isn't much that frustrates me faster. College hit all of my triggers.

I've never told my family about college. Just the broad strokes. They knew that most of the time I was only attending part-time. What they didn't know was how often I signed up for full-time classes but dropped down to one class when it got hard. I've never talked to any of them about how hard it was intellectually and emotionally. What I am the most ashamed about is how much time and money I wasted. Money that wasn't mine. Money that my parents spent. Maybe I would have treated it differently if it had been my money. Maybe not. I don't know, and it doesn't matter. I can't change the past.

Trying to make myself fit into the plan and expectations that my dad and society had for me was like trying to fit a square peg into a round hole. It just didn't work. I couldn't see that at the time. I just kept plugging away at it, thinking that was what adult life was like.

What finally changed? When my dad died, he left me enough money to make a pretty huge difference. I was free to do whatever I wanted with the money. I didn't have to answer to anyone about it. I didn't have to worry about what my dad, or anyone, would think. Was it a good investment? Would it be met with approval? Did I waste it on something frivolous? It didn't matter. It only mattered what I thought, and I tried to think carefully about what I spent the money on.

That money allowed me to study animal communication – something I've wanted to do since my twenties. The study program gave me practice and helped me gain confidence. I'm incredibly grateful that I had the money from my dad to do it! I like to think that he'd be proud of me. He might not understand it (he was an engineer after all!), but I think that he would be proud of me for finally finding something that I love.

Studying talking with animals was exciting. I'd wanted this for so long and I was finally doing it! I was nervous and exhilarated. There were

6-15 people all talking with the same animal then giving our results out loud to the whole class and getting feedback. It was like standing up to give a report in front of everyone. I'd start talking before my internal dialog had a chance to talk me out of it. Once I was done, the nerves were over and the excitement stayed. When my internal dialog tried to talk me into quitting, I'd simply ask, "What's your alternate plan for being an animal communicator?" and the voice quieted.

Talking with animals and their people is so satisfying. I've had animals say things to me that brought me to the height of love and joy, like the spider that spent a month trying to tell me he was my "friend." When I finally got it, it came with such love that it brought tears to my eyes. There was a young cat that told me that he might be the littlest in the family, but he was still in charge because he had the biggest attitude. There are animals near the end of their lives that may or may not want help crossing the rainbow bridge. Each animal that I talk to is beautiful. Each is different.

I'm not going to lie. It's not all sunshine and roses. I still have days when I struggle to get out of bed. If I'm honest, I have days when it's hard to get out of bed at all. I wonder if I am on the right path and doing the right thing. Building a business and client list is hard work. I know how I feel now as compared to how I felt back then. It's very different. This time, I don't feel like I'm going through the motions because I'm "supposed to." This time there is determination, satisfaction, and excitement.

I've had the opportunity to be in a group coaching program that has taught me volumes about myself and to accept myself more than I ever have before. I'm now in training to be a personal coach. Coaches have helped me transform my life, and I want to offer that to other people.

I'm writing. I've done a little traveling. I've been volunteering and relearning some skills that I hadn't practiced in a long time. I'm so much happier than I've been in a very long time.

Most of all, I'm learning to make the best decisions for *me*. Adulting is hard. I'm learning that it is okay, and necessary, to ask for help. It's not a weakness.

PATH TO YOUR POWER

Here are some things to think about if you identify with my story.

When do you procrastinate? Is it a particular activity like writing papers or essays, or is it any writing at all, even an email? Or maybe things that involve money? Interactions when you feel unsure of yourself?

What do you feel like when you procrastinate? For example, the closer I get to my deadline, the more pangs of fear I have, "I'm running out of time!" As time goes on, I start to feel constantly uneasy until I get the task done.

Everyone procrastinates sometimes and there are a variety of reasons. There might be a short-term relief from stress related to doing the thing. Long term, it tends to create even more stress as one becomes pressed for time or feels guilty for not doing the thing at all. If I notice that I am regularly procrastinating around a task, it's time for me to stop and find out why. If I'm putting things off, some part of me doesn't want to look at it, and I may need to ask for help from a coach or a therapist. These days, I really want to get to the root of the problem and heal it instead of quitting what's causing me stress like I used to.

____

____

____

____

Obligation can feel like a no-way-out scenario. If I feel obligated to do something, I need to give it a serious look. Why do I feel obligated? Who do I think that I owe, and why do I think that I owe them? Is this how I want to continue to live my life?

Another thing to think about: Did both parties agree to this obligation? Do you feel obligated because you had a conversation and agreed, or have you made an assumption about what the other person expects and taken this on yourself?

What is the worst thing that would happen if you didn't fulfill the obligation? How likely is that outcome to actually happen? Can you live with it if it does?

____

____

____

____

It's okay to go against others' expectations of you. Each of us gets to choose what we want to do and be in life. College isn't for everyone. It wasn't for me and that doesn't make me less of a person or less classy.

When it feels impossible, I tell myself, "I am *willing* to *try*." It doesn't have to be perfect. If it still feels too hard, I ask myself what *trying* would look like. The thing about trying is that it can be really small steps at a time. Even the smallest efforts count as trying. If I make more than one small effort, the effort adds up.

What is your goal that you are working on? What does trying look like for you? What small steps can you do daily, weekly, or monthly to move toward your goal? What are you going to do differently this time that you haven't done before?

____

____

____

____

ABOUT

With her second contribution to the *Behind the Power* book series, Jennifer Etzwiler continues to dance off-beat to life's music. She found non-traditional methods that work for her to live with depression. She is an intuitive healer and talks to animals, arachnids, and sometimes even people.

When Jennifer isn't filling the shoes of Dr. Doolittle, she can be found enjoying creative hobbies like sewing, knitting, and jewelry making. She also is frequently found on Zoom, helping others connect with each other and learn new things.

If you are curious about what your animal friend might be thinking or saying to the next-door neighbor's cat, then you can contact her through jenniferetzwiler.com.

Many Fairy Blessings!! ♡ Carri Betts

CHAPTER 11

BREAKING FREE

CARRI BETTS

On September 11, 2013 my life would change forever. I was having lunch with a friend when I received the phone call I had been dreading. When I answered I could hear the panic in my mother's voice as she yelled, "Carri, come quick, Tony shot himself!"

Everything went blank, but I managed to turn to my friend and let out the words, "Tony shot himself, we gotta get to my mom's right now." Barefoot and in my pajamas, with tears flowing down my face, my friend and I bolted out the door. Driving over I felt like I was going to throw up; my body was shaking and I could barely breathe. When I arrived at my mother's, she came running down the stairs to meet me at the door. There was panic in her voice, but she was surprisingly calm.

"He's in the basement and the police are on the way," she said. I ran downstairs to the basement and there he was–my beloved step-father who had become closer to me than my biological father ever was–and he was lying face down in a pool of blood with a shotgun under him. He was wearing his red and black plaid hunting jacket. Seeing him made me drop to my knees beside him. I put my face on his back, holding him. I felt the anger welling up and all I could do was scream at him, "Why would you do this!? Why!? Why!? We love you so much!" The next thing I knew the cops arrived to find me stuck to his lifeless body. I heard my mother's voice break through my uncontrollable sobs.

"Come on, Carri, he's gone, you have to let go." But I couldn't let go, I didn't want to. I knew I would never be able to hug him again. Finally, the officer on duty had to remove me. He took me outside where I collapsed to the ground, sobbing, and screaming. As I sat in the grass I thought, *OH FUCK!!! Adelaide is about to be let out of school. She's supposed to walk here today. I cannot let her walk around the corner to see the ambulance and police car parked outside her grandparents' apartment.* I got myself together as much as I could and had my friend drive me over to the Junior High to pick up my daughter.

Walking into the school, I felt a little crazy as my head was spinning and I couldn't breathe. I went straight into the principal's office. He happened to be my old high school history teacher so he knew me and our family well. He took one look at me and said, "Carri, what's wrong?"

I could barely get the words out, "I need to get Adelaide, Tony shot himself." His jaw dropped open and tears came out of his eyes as he made the call to dismiss her to the office. As I sat there waiting for my daughter, my whole body was trembling, I had a lump in my throat, and all I could think about was how I was going to tell my sweet, innocent girl that her Tony was gone.

The principal could see me in a spiral of emotions. He asked me what I needed and reassured me he would help us get through this. When Adelaide stepped into the office, she took one look at me and knew something was wrong. I immediately wrapped my arms around her.

"Pumpkin, Grampy shot himself, he's gone." I had to fight to get the words out of my mouth. She almost crumbled to the ground. Holding each other up, we rushed out of the school as the hall was filling up with kids.

"Mom, I heard the sirens go by when I was in class and had a feeling they were going to Mimi's house," she cried into my arms as we got in the car. My heart broke all over again. We returned to my mother's apartment where Adelaide's nana, her father's mom, was waiting for us so she could watch her while I went to the funeral home with my mother. I was on autopilot doing what needed to be done, so much so that the next several hours were a blur. When I returned home Adelaide was already asleep in her room. As I sat on the living room couch feeling completely out of my body all I could do was yell at God and ask him *why.*

"Why, God? Why? Why would he do this, how could he do this to us!?" I couldn't stop screaming and sobbing realizing that my friend, who was more of a father to me than my own, was gone and I would never see him again.

Tony had been struggling with depression after the loss of his nephew Nick to suicide a couple years prior. He spent most days at my house due to the amount of work that needed to be done. Even if he wasn't fixing up the house he would be out in my yard, either gardening, working on some project, or pondering his thoughts. On the days I would help him, we would typically get involved in deep conversation with many tears being shed by us both, as I could feel his pain. In fact, he even told me he wanted to see the dark place his dear Nick went.

Losing his nephew changed the person whom we all knew and loved dearly. He was drowning his pain in alcohol to the point I had to remove all the alcohol from my own home. He was becoming angry and talking in riddles which was not who he was at all.

Tony was always a very happy-go-lucky kind of guy with a deep chuckle. He was kind, loving, and would give the shirt off his back for anyone, whether he knew them or not. It was heartbreaking and scary for me to watch. Not only was I losing my best friend, my "dad," the one pivotal person that taught me about life, it also triggered memories of growing up with an alcoholic father. His drinking and behavior would cause me to pull away and become angry at him. I was terrified and hopeless as I watched him spiral out of control for two years.

After Tony died I found myself waking up expecting to see him in my backyard either working or grabbing tools out of the shed. Each morning when I looked out my bedroom window and didn't see him my world would be shattered. This was real, he was really gone. For the next year I would wake up looking for him, being ripped open day after day. The questions would start all over again and my thoughts got the best of me. I became numb, angry, and I was full of shame and guilt. I beat myself up on a daily basis. My internal dialogue told me it was all my fault. *You should've been able to save him. The signs were there and you just turned your back on him, you're such a piece of shit, Carri.-*

I knew I needed to find some strength to be there for my daughter and my mother. As I ignored my emotions to get through each day, just trying to be there for them, I started lashing out, and part of my trauma response was to become very attached to my daughter. Losing Tony triggered the abandonment issues I already had from my parents' divorce, which kicked my codependency into high gear. My fear of losing Adelaide caused me to have absolutely no boundaries with her. I projected my life onto her and leaned on her for everything, causing her to be "the parent" in many situations. Basically, it felt like we were two teenagers hanging out most of the time. My grief ran so deep that I couldn't emotionally be there for anyone, not even for myself. In fact, it was so deep I didn't even know what to do with it. Most days I found myself aimlessly wandering around outside, starting one project only to move to the next without completing any of them.

To be in silence was torture, as my mind would replay every conversation Tony and I had had over the past two years. I found distraction from those thoughts through music so I always had my headphones on, letting the music drown my pain. I was drinking more and even started using drugs again after years of being clean. My family could see the pain I was in, but instead of being supportive they thought it would be helpful to tell me to stop playing the victim. This only made things worse, making me feel like I had to ignore my feelings even more. Quite honestly it made me feel like I wasn't being seen or heard.

My life was completely spinning out of control. I was pushing everyone away and lost many friends. I finally realized I needed help so I found a therapist who was non-judgmental and who finally listened.

My mother suggested going to a suicide survivors' support group together which was offered through hospice. Although I was reluctant to go it was one of the most healing things I did for myself. Being a part of the group allowed me to feel my feelings and realize I wasn't alone on this journey. I learned how to honor not only my feelings but Tony's memory as well.

One day in my support group someone recommended doing something that our loved ones liked to do in order to honor them and connect with them. Tony loved to garden, so I decided I would try my hand at it. With my headphones on, I got to work digging in the dirt creating lots of flower beds. Little did I know how healing this would be. As I dug in the dirt, listening to music, day after day, sobbing and screaming, releasing the pain into the earth, I would slowly start to heal. The more time I spent in the soil, the more I felt connected to him. In fact, I even heard him chuckle at me more than once.

Over time I was able to take my headphones out and just be with nature, and this would allow the most amazing thing to happen. I could hear the flowers like I did when I was a child, bringing a sense of renewal to my purpose and intuitive abilities. Every morning and evening I would sit under my willow tree that Tony planted when I moved into my house, and she would bring me great comfort while allowing me to feel connected to Tony. Eventually I would start to hear his voice more and more. One day, as I was gardening, I heard him just like he was there helping me.

"Bear, I am so sorry for the pain I caused you and Adelaide. My pain was just too deep; please forgive me. I love you so much and I am proud of you." The more I talked with him, the more signs I received from him and the louder his voice became.

As time passed from months to years, I eventually developed the sense that I could not stay in my home if I wanted to continue to heal. The memories had me in shackles and the shame and guilt were holding me back, even with all the work I was doing to heal in coaching programs and through spiritual meditations and guidance. I felt I owed it to everyone to stay. *Who was I to find happiness after all we had been through?*

My daughter was expecting her first born, so of course I wanted to be there for that, but the energy was getting heavier by the day. I was starting to hear Tony nudging me out, telling me it was time for me to live my dreams, that I had sacrificed enough and it was time for me to find true happiness. Although I felt I was trapped in my own home, I also felt if I left I would lose my connection with him.

It all became clear one Friday night as I was lying in bed when my ears started ringing. It was a high-pitched frequency that came from nowhere. My entire body started shaking and my stomach was in knots. I thought, *OH Shit!! What are my guides trying to tell me?!?* I heard them loud and clear. They were telling me it was time to leave the house I had been living in for the past ten years. That there was no way I could heal fully if I stayed, and the ties must be broken.

The sense of urgency to leave made me feel unsafe and, quite honestly, made me feel a little crazy. It felt as though someone was out to bury me either spiritually, physically, or emotionally. The truth is I was already dying a little inside every day by staying there.

Day after day I found myself on the floor of this house, sobbing uncontrollably and feeling like I was being ripped in half by grief. Although my family was all around me I felt lonely, unwanted, unheard, and unloved. I knew I had to leave but was resisting what my body was telling me. The push from my guides was just what I needed. The next morning I awoke feeling frantic, sad, and terrified. I packed what Spirit guided me to take as fast as I could, grabbed my dog and set off with no real plan in place. I only had a thousand dollars in my wallet as I drove away, leaving everyone and everything I knew behind.

The tears flowed down my face as I realized how much trauma that house was holding. A house that was once full of so much love had become cold, empty, and full of sadness because Tony's energy permeated every square inch of those walls. He had been here with me almost every single day for years up until his passing, and I could feel the memories of him constantly; not letting go was a beautiful part of my grieving, but it was also suffocating me and holding me back from releasing my own pain. I was finally able to see that leaving was the best thing I could do for myself; sometimes it is necessary in life to let go of things and people we love in order to grow and heal.

As I continue to heal in my new environment and embrace life as an empath I am finding compassion for myself and discovering who I truly am without the influence of others. This journey to personal freedom has been full of ups and downs and has been terrifying at times. It has taken a lot of inner work towards finding the light that lies within the darkness of all the loss I had experienced over the past ten years. I have learned to not take things or people for granted, to have not only compassion for myself but with others, and it drove me to reconnect with the love I have always felt from Mother Earth, as she is the one who will always support me, love me unconditionally, and help me continue to heal.

PATH TO YOUR POWER

If you've lost a loved one to suicide it is possible to heal the deep pain you are experiencing. I know it seems dark, confusing, and like you could've done more to help save them. The thing is, their pain was their pain and it was too much for them to bear; it was not due to something you did or said. The shame and guilt you feel only adds to the grief leaving you feeling broken, angry, and like you can't move on. Healing this loss will take lots of self work, time, and support. You must allow yourself grace, forgiveness of self and your loved one. It is also important to feel your feelings, recognize your emotions and release them. I found keeping a journal that I used to write to my stepdad every day helped tremendously.

Find a therapist, one whom you trust and feel comfortable with. I highly encourage you to find a suicide survivors' support group where you can share with people who are going through the same thing you are.

Connect with nature, go on long walks, sit under a tree, look up at the sky. Still have conversations with your loved one on the other side; they will hear you.

Lastly, do things to honor them. Honoring them can look like doing things that you liked to do together. Taking a moment of silence. And one of my favorite things to do is a simple little candle ritual.

Set up an altar with pictures and things that remind you of them or even things of theirs. In the middle of your altar place a plate. On that plate you will place a white or pink candle; I like to use both. Create a circle around the candles with sea salt – this is for protection and will absorb any negative energies. Next, take some rose petals and scatter them around the candles on the plate – this will provide love and comfort. You will need two pieces of rose quartz and two pieces of black tourmaline. Take your rose quartz and place it in the east and west of the plate. The tourmaline will be placed in the north and south. Before lighting the candles burn a little sage to cleanse the space and call in the four cardinal directions north, south, east, west and all spaces in between – this will create a sacred circle around you. Ask your angels to communicate any messages you may have to your loved one and vice versa. When lighting the candles you can say today I honor you, I am grateful for the time on earth we shared, your presence is never gone as our hearts will always be connected. May we reach deep to mend the wounds from this loss. And so it is.

ABOUT

Carri Betts is a magical Fairy of wonder who inspires others to find the light in the midst of their darkness. As a best-selling author and speaker of Behind the Power, Carri encourages you to look deep within so you can reach your full potential and realize your mistakes don't define you. As an intuitive healer she uses her profound wisdom to select the most effective healing path for both people and animals. Holding certifications in Emotional Freedom Technique (tapping), Reiki, and Flower Therapy, she guides clients every step of the way with kindness, compassion, and grace. As a resin artist, Carri uses her intuition to custom design pyramids layered with the healing properties of nature to purify, cleanse, and provide continuous healing in your space. She is also profoundly gifted intuitively using all of her gifts and talents to light the path for everyone she serves.

To learn more about Carri and her services visit https://carribetts.com/.

Get radical and love yourself. Kristi Ferrise

CHAPTER 12

HEALING THROUGH RADICAL SELF-COMPASSION

KRISTI MITCHAM-FERRISE

Have you ever found yourself alone and crying because of an overwhelming fear and sadness that takes over? That's my story. The crazy thing about this is most people who know me would think that I have it all together and am a genuinely happy person. My hope is that you'll find something in my story that you can relate to and know that you can get through these moments of despair. Not just get through them but heal them.

I appeared to be happy most of my life. No one knew the fear and sadness inside. Throughout my life, I learned to hide and act like everything was okay. I truly cared about others and encouraged them to get through hard times. Re-directing attention from me to others allowed me to avoid my fear and sadness that I experienced when I was alone. Anything that prevented me from healing was a choice. This is a form of hiding, and I started hiding at a very young age. Being the fifth child, and the baby, I got a lot of attention. My world changed when my little brother was born three years after me. I remember when my mom brought my little brother home from the hospital. I noticed that he received all of the attention. I noticed how

I felt like I had been replaced, so I learned to play by myself. I learned to be independent.

As an adult, I didn't understand why these dark feelings sometimes crept in. My life didn't seem so bad. I had a successful career, good friends, and love interests. However, when I was alone, I felt so sad and would just cry. I hid this from my parents, my friends, my lovers, even myself. Every traumatic experience I'd had either taught me a new skill of how to hide better, or how to react...which was not always a good thing. I let each traumatic experience build upon negative thoughts and confirm to myself that I could easily be cast aside. I became very familiar with this feeling of total despair when I was alone. I believed that I did not matter. I believed that I did not deserve happiness because it would be taken away from me. So, I preferred to heal others instead of myself.

I was molested when I was eleven years old by a distant family member. I kept asking him to tickle me because I wanted attention, but his mind and intentions were in a place my innocent mind could not understand. My adolescent brain couldn't process what was happening; one minute he was tickling me and the next he was fondling me and making me feel incredibly unsafe. When it happened, he gaslit me and said nothing was going on. My mind was racing. *I can't disrespect him. Why is this happening? Maybe he has the right to do this to me? I have to get away. I'll tell him that my sister needs me. I feel dirty. Maybe I can take a shower and erase everything that happened. Could I be pregnant? Let me scrub the sensations away. My mom wants to know why I'm showering in the middle of the day. I'll lie to her and tell her I just wanted to. It worked! I can never tell anyone. They won't believe me. I must have done something to make him want to do this to me. I don't know what I did. I don't like this. Why me? I have to get away. I did something wrong. This is my fault. I want to hide. I don't ever want to see him again. What will I do when he comes back?* I had no way of knowing how to deal with these thoughts. Resources for sexual assault didn't exist then like they do now. So, years of listening to these thoughts made me feel that I could be easily cast aside. I felt like I did not matter. I believed that I couldn't tell my secret.

When I was sixteen years old, we moved from California to Colorado. For a teenager, moving can be a traumatic event. I left my friends behind. My life as I knew it changed. I did not have any control over this move. It once again confirmed my feeling that I didn't matter. I was very depressed and hid this from my parents. In fact, one day, my mom raised concerns about my little brother because he was acting out and wasn't fitting in with his new school and friends. When she asked me to keep an eye out for him, I remember thinking that I didn't matter because she didn't know that I was struggling as well. I appeared to be fine, but every night, I would write a letter to no one and explain why I did not want to be here anymore, how I didn't matter, and cry myself to sleep. I chose to not say anything to my parents. I thought that my brother mattered more than me, so I stayed silent. I learned to hide my emotions and make it appear like everything was fine. At this point in life, it was normal for me to be concerned for others more than myself.

Nine years after the molestation, the first person I told was my best friend from college. I told her on our annual drive to Myrtle Beach. She heard me and didn't judge. She just listened. I felt safe enough with her to give her details. She loved me so much and she was angry at the person that did this to me. She cared about me. This was the first time that I completely opened up to someone. She accepted me, even though I had been ashamed of what happened to me. She helped me feel safe. She let me talk it all out. My friend believed me and it was a relief. I began to go to counseling.

With my newfound courage that I received from telling my friend and the counseling, I went on to tell my five siblings about the molestation. My brothers didn't have much to say. Now, I can think of a million reasons why. Back then we didn't talk about anything like this. You see, I was raised in a very protective religious environment. It was normal to hide anything bad because I saw that people would judge and I certainly didn't want to be judged or accused of anything. My one sister accused me of lying. My other sister, whom I am closest to, cried with me and began to question parts of her childhood that she blocked out. My sister-in-law was angry that I didn't tell them sooner because her children had been alone with this man. I felt like each time I told someone, the attention immediately went away from me and back to how it affected them. I still felt like I didn't matter even though I was finally speaking my truth. In my late twenties, I did write my parents a six-page letter explaining why throughout my life I had never liked male doctors, and why I always appeared to be a loner. I didn't tell them who molested me, but I did tell them that it happened. I asked for a few weeks to process my emotions of letting my secret out. Several weeks after I gave them the letter, we met for breakfast and my parents let me know that they loved me and the letter gave them some answers as to why I made the decisions that I did in my life.

"I can't imagine who would have done this to you," my mom said, heartbroken and angry. She asked me who molested me and I told her that she didn't want to know; she never asked me again, and we never spoke about my trauma. I was okay with this because I didn't want to hurt anyone or bring up any emotions that could have caused enormous trauma. I did feel like I wasn't judged, and it felt good to tell my parents. I felt accepted. However, even though I finally told people, I wasn't healed and I wasn't ready to start the work toward healing either.

In my twenties, I was in a small group counseling session with other people that had been molested. I remember this like it was yesterday. One girl in our group told me that I didn't belong there because my molestation was not as violent as hers. I immediately felt ashamed and wanted to go back into hiding. One side of me felt ashamed that my trauma wasn't "as bad" as hers. Another part of me felt guilty that I was making a big deal about my trauma. I sat through countless therapy sessions where I was asked to relive my trauma and "talk it out," but this method did not heal my shame and guilt. Talking about it with my counselors just caused me to relive the trauma. I did not heal the negative thoughts that I listened to consistently for the nine years of hiding my secret. I still believed that I could be easily cast aside.

In my thirties, I had an amazing job working for a large private pension company. I was very successful. My managers recognized my skill and effort. I went on to become a Team Leader and helped to open a regional office in Denver. Eventually, our department grew and we needed to hire another Team Leader. Things were great, until one day, my co-worker received recognition for something that I thought was a team effort. Now I am sure she deserved this recognition, but it was how I processed this event that caused me to revert back to my shame and guilt. I will never forget the shock on my team's faces when she received this award instead of me. I went to the bathroom and cried. In my mind, I was cast aside and didn't deserve the recognition. I was triggered and this event brought back the shame and guilt from when I was younger. It bothered me enough to leave my position as Team Leader to pursue a career that would fulfill me more without realizing that, once again, I was running and hiding from my pain, and I was deciding to throw action at the problem instead of fixing the root cause of my pain.

I am now in my early fifties. I didn't just wake up and decide that I needed help one day. It took another traumatic experience to force me to work on my healing.

I met my husband in 2004. Our life together was amazing. Our love for the water, boating, fishing, and lobstering brought us together even more. Being on the boat with him was my happy place. We were present with each other when we were together. I had never experienced such love with a man. He protected me and that made me feel safe. I now realize that I pushed away from healing and avoided dealing with my fears and sadness because I thought that I didn't need to anymore. We had each other. He accepted me, even though he didn't know that I had a deep wound that needed to be healed. I will admit that when he went fishing with his friends, I would stay at home and just cry. I would let the shame and guilt creep in and take over. I was still hiding even though my life seemed amazing. It *was* amazing. However, when I was alone I was reliving my trauma as though it just happened. When my husband came home, I would wipe my tears and my wonderful life would resume.

My husband passed away in August 2017 after a 20-month battle fighting cancer. My world was frozen. My safety was taken away and I was vulnerable again. This feeling was all too familiar and I couldn't take it anymore. I was tired of this repeated pattern and knew that I needed help, but I felt defeated. I still had my shame and guilt. I still had my fear and sadness. I was not healed.

Today, I am choosing to heal. I am giving myself the compassion that I longed for my entire life. I no longer cry when I am alone. I have been given the tools to use to work through my thought process, which has allowed me to heal the parts of me that were still in pain. I have learned to change my thoughts about my experiences. For example, the day I was molested, my mom was entertaining guests and had five other children to take care of. It wasn't that I wasn't important, she just had a lot of other responsibilities to deal with and what happened to me went unnoticed by no fault of her own. When our family moved to Colorado, I chose to not say anything about how difficult it was for me. I have now forgiven myself for thinking that I had to deal with this alone. I never let them know that I was suffering, too, so how could they help if they didn't know? When I wrote the letter to my parents telling them everything about my life, I am sure that they were shocked. But they did give me my space and did talk with me when I was ready. Through counseling, I have learned that there are different types of trauma, but how we think and feel about our trauma can have a major impact on how we live. For that co-worker that stole my thunder… she did not steal my thunder. If anything, I am proud of her and know that I contributed to her success. We were quite the team. I know that I would have been rewarded when the time came, and that outlook comes from the work I have done and continue to do with Allyson.

I am so proud of how far I've come. I don't think I'm crazy anymore. I am pretty powerful. My thoughts can knock me down or build me up. I choose to build myself up and it feels amazing. You too can heal.

If we discount our own pain, or punish ourselves for feeling lost, scared or alone, then we are choosing to not heal. We are not seeing our choices. We are judging ourselves and not giving ourselves the compassion that we wish we'd had when we were younger. We are not victims any longer. I don't want you to hear my story and say that your own suffering is less significant or more traumatic. I want you to believe that if I can do it, then so can you. Instead of asking, "Why me?" start to ask, "What now?"

PATH TO YOUR POWER

I learned to acknowledge the feelings associated with what was going on through the method of thought models. Allyson is a big proponent of this method in her coaching. Once I acknowledge the feelings, I can work through my reaction and change the result. I started off small, got in the habit of doing this almost daily, and eventually saw the positive result. Cognitive therapy has helped me to understand how to change my thoughts about a circumstance so that the end result is more positive. For example, here was my thought process about my molestation:

	Past	Present
Circumstance	I was molested.	I was molested.
Thoughts	I did something to deserve this. I am ashamed. This will happen again.	It will not happen again. I made a good choice when I was eleven to get away. I am proud of that girl.
Feelings	I am afraid.	I feel good about my choices/glad.
Action	I live in fear so I hide.	Doing the work daily.
Result	I've lived in fear my whole life and have not healed.	I am proud of how far I've come and how much I've healed.

Now try to complete your own thought model:

	Past	**Present**
Circumstance		
Thoughts		
Feelings		
Action		
Result		

When you are finished, ask yourself some follow-up questions, and begin to plan a reasonable course of action based on how you truly FEEL and not what you think is the "right" decision or the one that will win approval from others.

ABOUT

Kristi Ferrise was born and raised in the bay area of Northern California. She has lived in Colorado, Virginia, New York and now Marathon, FL.

Kristi had a successful corporate career where she worked for a large private pension company in Denver, Colorado. In 2001, she relocated to Marathon, FL where she worked at the Dolphin Research Center.

Her most recent career has been teaching. She taught Kindergarten for over ten years and now teaches Middle and High School Art in Florida.

Love & Blessings ♡
Karen

CHAPTER 13

BECOMING MY OWN SOULMATE

KAREN THOMAS

As I lay in the gurney in the Emergency Room, I could not keep my eyes open. The stabbing pain through my right eye felt like an ice pick was lodged between my eye and the back of my head. As much as I tried to manage this progressively building headache over the past several days, I finally surrendered to it when I could no longer function.

As I waited for the physician to examine me, I created stories in my mind about what might be happening to me. Oh God, what if I'm having a stroke? This can't be happening. I don't want to be a burden on anyone. I don't want anyone to have to take care of me. I am a nurse. It's my duty to care for others, not the other way around.

After eight hours of intense pain I was finally taken for a CT scan and X-rays. The results frightened me: a blood clot in my head and a broken rib. I needed to be admitted. I was scared. I cried silently while I rehearsed the details of a believable story that I could tell my parents when I finally got the courage to call them.

Earlier that week I was sleeping soundly when I heard the lock to my apartment door rattling around 2 AM. The locks had recently been changed by maintenance, and I had not given a copy of the new key to anyone. My heart started racing and instinctively I knew it was Brent, the man I had been seeing for the past several months. I could feel his rage as he easily and forcefully came through the door. I laid in bed perfectly still and said a short prayer for my safety. Brent stormed into my bedroom, ripped the covers off of me, and grabbed me by my neck. "Who are you fucking?!" he raged, his bloodshot eyes open wide with intense anger. I could smell alcohol on his breath, and another woman's perfume on his clothes.

"What are you talking about?" I pleaded, trying to stay as calm as possible. I took a blow to my head, and the next thing I remember I woke up on the bathroom floor. My head was throbbing, and my vision was blurry. I felt nauseated, and it really hurt to take a deep breath. I sat on the cold tile floor with my back against the wall trying to make sense out of what just happened. Everything was still. Brent was gone, and I was alive.

How did this just happen? What did I do to make Brent so angry and jealous? How am I going to hide these injuries from people?

I had a history of dating men that were emotionally and verbally abusive. I grew up in a household where that was the norm, and women were disrespected in general. Brent was the first man, however, to repeatedly harm me physically.

I was admitted to the hospital for ten days, then sent home on blood thinners. I was given the very specific instruction of "do not get pregnant," since the risk of severe side effects to a fetus was very high. I had zero boundaries so I did not say no when Brent came back around for sex. Eight weeks later I found myself sitting in an abortion clinic waiting for my turn. I carried that shame and guilt of aborting my child for almost two decades.

My patterns continued; I was comfortable being treated with disrespect, and subconsciously I didn't feel worthy of anything better. I was getting attention and physical affection through sex. I was financially independent, lived alone, and kept my family at arm's length. On the outside I appeared to be a happy, successful, independent woman. On the inside I was simply a dying prisoner of my own mind; I lived a life of secrets, careful not to discuss the shameful details of my personal life at work, around family members, or the few friends I had.

When I was in college, I was hyper vigilant about what others thought about me, and desperately tried to fit in with the popular crowd. I longed for love, validation, and acceptance from others. When I wasn't studying and striving for perfect grades, I was searching for that 'perfect person' to complete me, which I sought through drinking too much at parties and sleeping with strangers. I felt like an empty vessel, desperately trying to fill that deep, endless black hole inside of me.

I was on the verge of tears most of the time, 'homesick' for something other than my home, and felt uncomfortable in my own skin. I was constantly comparing myself to others and was convinced that I wasn't thin enough or pretty enough for anyone to completely love me.

I had a habit of dating men that were married, in a relationship, or otherwise emotionally unavailable. I learned to keep family secrets from a very young age, so this felt natural to me. I was walking through life without a moral compass, manipulating, and hurting people along the way. I carried this cloak of shame for many years as well.

When I was 41, my chiropractor recommended I start working with the personal trainer who was working out of her office so I could strengthen my legs after persistent leg injuries I sustained from years of overexercising, and that very day I was introduced to Mariah.

She was tall, athletic, and carried herself with confidence. When she reached out her hand to shake mine, I felt this electric warmth run up my arm and through my body. She held steady eye contact as I was explaining what I needed help with. Her eyes were the color of Tiger's eye gemstone – deep, rich, and piercing. I felt like she was staring into my soul.

After our sessions we would spend time talking about our lives. We had so much in common: dysfunctional families, growing up with abuse, drugs, and alcohol, deep love of dogs, similar exercise routines, a love for the beach, traveling, and past romantic partners who were emotionally abusive. Mariah completely understood me. She was fully engaged and present with me, and all without judgment. I felt completely safe. I felt like I could breathe again.

I couldn't stop thinking about Mariah which felt so strange. I never dated a woman before, nor felt this sexual attraction to a woman. I was completely conflicted, but I knew I wanted to explore this. It wasn't long before Mariah embraced me in a warm, long, tight hug, which I could have stayed in for the rest of my life. For the first time in my life I felt safe. I was seen and heard. I was validated. I knew in my heart she was the one. Knowing the universe worked in mysterious ways, it didn't take long for me to accept the fact that my true love showed up in female form. I did not share my feelings openly, however, for fear of judgment and ridicule from others.

Within a few months, I fell deeply in love and made the decision to finally embrace a loving and monogamous relationship with Mariah. I could feel the uneasiness in my family and among the few friends that I had, but that became less important to me. It was now 'us against the world.' Through my eyes Mariah could do no wrong. She rescued me during a low point in my life and quickly pointed out the ways in which my dysfunctional family was still hurting me. Mariah seemed to have this deep wisdom about my past abuse and understood my pain. She knew about my lifelong struggle with eating disorders and body image, and chose to love and support me anyway.

Mariah put me on a pedestal telling me daily how beautiful, perfect, and angelic I was. She often referred to me as a "unicorn." She started buying me flowers weekly and surprising me with gifts. We quickly moved in together. Three months after we started dating she planned a big birthday party for me, celebrating me simply because I exist. My birthday became her favorite day of the year, and she affectionately called me her "favorite" and her "twin flame." We explored spirituality together through books, meditations, workshops, and Native American sweat lodges. We felt like we knew each other for lifetimes. I had finally met the mirror image of my soul. I knew we were eternally bound and reunited once again.

I was given more attention than I had ever received in my life. Since I was completely starved of attention before Mariah, I absorbed it like a dry sponge. We exchanged words like "forever," "always," and, "eternity," all of which felt safe and completely true. It felt like a fairy tale romance, and I believed every word of the script. Mariah and I would often talk about what our happily-ever-after life would look like. We'd live on a large farm with lots of dogs and animals, living off of the land and our love for each other.

Within the first six months of our relationship we were completely enmeshed with each other and inseparable. I unknowingly handed over all of my power and was deep in codependency, which of course I did not recognize at the time. I let Mariah make all of the decisions in our relationship. Even if something didn't feel right, I was unable to identify my feelings, so I stayed quiet. I lacked boundaries and self-esteem. I felt overly responsible for Mariah's feelings, and her moods dictated how my day went. When she was happy, so was I, and our life felt joyous. When she was angry about something, I became very anxious trying to fix what she was angry about. Life felt like a roller coaster ride, which to me felt perfectly normal.

Over the years Mariah and I experienced amazing trips together, traveling the country with our dogs. She held my hand through my breast cancer journey; supporting, loving, and helping me heal. I thanked God every day for giving me this incredible gift after years of enduring abusive and empty relationships.

Embracing the fluidity of my sexuality, I enjoyed being intimate with a woman. Maybe that was the problem all of these years?

Aha, that was it!! All of my relationships had failed because men couldn't relate to me and would ultimately disrespect me. Being with a woman was different. I felt safe and understood.

Our seemingly happy lives were forever changed in 2017 after a devastating hurricane tore through our town. The next two years were spent trying to rebuild our lives while living in a small, borrowed trailer parked in my mother's yard. Depression slowly set in on Mariah, while I stayed extremely busy to avoid confronting it.

I felt the distance between us, but I continued to try to make everything right again. I prayed often for divine intervention to help me repair everything. From my perspective it was my fault that we had problems and I was desperate to fix it. As increasing disdain towards my mother stressed our relationship, Mariah desperately wanted to move out of her yard. I was agreeable to do anything to make her happy and get back to the bliss we once shared.

Over the course of two years I willingly paid for rent at two different apartments (one located fifty miles away) so Mariah could have her 'space.' I also kept up with the mortgage on a home that was destroyed. I also took out a disaster loan to pay a construction company to rebuild our home. This company later filed for bankruptcy and skipped town with my loan money. I was at an all-time low at this point and just when I thought things couldn't get worse, Mariah decided to move to the apartment fifty miles away so she could have space from everything.

When I would go visit her for 'date nights' it was clear that she was simply no longer interested in me. I persisted for months to try to repair our relationship. I blamed myself for this void between us, beating myself up daily for allowing it to get to this point. Even though the writing was on the wall, I was still shocked and devastated to learn that she had found a new romantic partner a few months after moving. It took me a very long time to comprehend that the one person who said they would never leave me, left.

I was alone with a shattered heart, shattered dreams, and over $300,000 in debt to my name. In that moment of deep despair, I declared myself forever unlovable by humans, and unworthy of any good fortune. I'd been rejected by my 'twin flame.' I was convinced that the only true love that existed for me was with my dogs, who have been there for me my entire life.

If I had the vocabulary at the time, I would have referred to this relationship as a classic narcissistic/codependent dance that lasted almost eight years. But I didn't have the insight to recognize this relationship for what it was. As I reflect back on it a quote from Maya Angelou comes to mind: "Do the best you can until you know better. Then when you know better, do better."

I wasn't able to recognize my life-long codependency until I was alone, drowning in my grief. This is when I was introduced to the work of two different life coaches, one being Allyson Roberts. I learned that my patterns of behavior were the result of childhood programming. I was starting to understand my distorted belief system about myself. I discovered why I'd been attracting partners that abused me, whether overtly or covertly. Most importantly, I discovered how badly I was abusing myself.

Through consistent self-work with Cognitive Behavioral Therapy (which can be grueling at times) I was able to rise above my despair and challenge my limiting beliefs. I've experienced that healing happens in layers. Once an old pattern is recognized and can be worked on, another old pattern would surface. Rewiring fifty-two years of faulty programming takes time, persistence, and patience.

I find the healing work is challenging and never actually complete. I stayed numb for most of my life through eating disorders and disassociating from my body in times of stress. Now I'm consciously staying in my body and processing my emotions, which is a learning curve. I still have to remind myself to have patience and grace while I'm healing, as I can struggle and strive at the same time.

My life now focuses much more on self-love, self-compassion, and self-respect. I've created boundaries with myself and others. I've learned how to say no to things I don't want, and yes to things that bring me joy. I'm learning to verbalize my needs and pursue my dreams. I'm no longer seeking outside validation or taking things personally. It feels amazing to stand in my own personal power. Is it perfect? No. But I'm willing to continue to do the work and be the best version of myself possible.

If I had to rewrite my story I wouldn't change a thing. I'm grateful for the spiritual growth that has come out of all of it. To this day I'm continuing to break the chains that bind me and continuing to grow. For the first time in my life I truly believe that I am lovable, and it all started with finally loving myself.

PATH TO YOUR POWER

I spent most of my life unaware that I lacked self-love and was therefore looking for outside validation to 'complete me.' I truly believed my happiness came from other people and circumstances. With this mindset it's been very easy to fall into the trap of predator-type personalities who were looking for someone to be their next target.

Here are some **red flags** to be aware of when beginning a new relationship with someone, romantic or not. These are just a few examples of unhealthy patterns which can be very subtle or very obvious.

> **Love Bombing** – In the beginning of a relationship with someone who has high narcissistic traits, it's common to experience this. Love bombing is a form of emotional manipulation in which an unhealthy person "bombs" you with an over-the-top amount of affection, flattery, gifts, and praise early in the relationship in order to win over your attention. The person usually presents as charming, successful, charismatic, and attractive. They may pedestalize you, claim their love for you, and make you feel like the luckiest person alive. Sadly, the motive behind this behavior is to ultimately control you.
>
> **Gaslighting** – This is an insidious form of emotional abuse that makes you question your beliefs and perceptions of reality. When someone is gaslighting you, you may second-guess yourself, your memories, recent events, and your perceptions. They may say things like: "You're making things up," "I never said that" or "You're crazy."

After this twisted conversation you may be left feeling confused and wondering if there is something wrong with you. You may end up feeling insecure, blame yourself, and apologizing for something you haven't done.

'Self-Serving' Empathy or Compassion – These individuals may seemingly have compassion for someone and will try to rescue them in an attempt to gain applause and recognition. If they don't receive praise or admiration for their sacrifice, they may feel bitter and resentful and comment about how people take advantage and don't appreciate them.

Sense of Entitlement – People with high narcissistic traits expect favorable treatment because they consider themselves special. They truly believe that whatever they want, they deserve to get. They also expect the people around them to automatically comply with their every whim. If you don't, you may be considered useless and be discarded.

Blame-shifting – This occurs when an unhealthy person does something wrong or inappropriate and then blames someone else to avoid taking responsibility for their own behavior. If they talk about how 'all of their exes were crazy' this is a warning sign. People on the narcissistic spectrum have an extremely difficult time taking accountability for their actions.

If you recognize any or a combination of these patterns within your relationships, you are not alone. Here are some resources that may offer support.

YouTube Channels:

- Lisa A. Romano Breakthrough Life Coach Inc.
- Dr. Ramani
- Dr. Todd Grande

Podcasts:

- Narcissism Recovery Podcast
- Narcissist Apocalypse
- The Virtual Couch Podcast: Waking up to Narcissism

ABOUT

Karen Thomas is a registered nurse, animal communicator, intuitive healer, and best-selling author. She combines her knowledge of a thirty-year nursing career with energy work and holistic methods to help homeless dogs with medical needs. As the founder of Payton's Promise, a nonprofit organization that provides sanctuary for dogs nearing end of life, or that have special needs, she has found her true passion and life calling.

Find out more about her at paytonspromisesanctuary.com.

CHAPTER 14

CHOOSING CURIOSITY OVER COMPULSION

BETH NAGLE GRIFFIN

It's very early Spring in 1968. I am four years old and I am glad to be out of Mrs. Reed's gray station wagon packed with loud kids. She drives us to and from preschool every day. With no seatbelts to restrain us, the back of the wagon is a rowdy scrum. Mrs. Reed pretends not to notice the chaos of hurtful shoves and pokes from other kids. I survived another ride home.

The walkway leads to the front stairs of our house. I turn the doorknob of the heavy glass and oak door, and step inside. Our German Shepherd Yo-Yo greets me with tail-wags. Next will be hugs and kisses from Nana and lunch, but I realize something is different. Everything is quiet. My nana is always here when I come home. Sometimes Mom is home, too. I feel panic. *Everyone has left! Is it because the orphanage that my brothers are always calling on the phone to come and take me back because I am not supposed to be here didn't come and get me fast enough? Is it because I cry too much and Mom doesn't like a cry-baby or because I am a "mistake?"*

Yo-Yo is here. She didn't leave. We are all alone. It's lunchtime and I need to figure things out quickly, so I manage to feed Yo-Yo. I am too small to open her can of smelly Alpo so I put leftover beans and cinnamon bread from the refrigerator into her dish. I twine my small hand tightly around her metal choke collar.

Yo-Yo is not interested in her lunch so I tug her to the living room. I put her on the couch with me which is really bad. She is not allowed in the living room or on any furniture, but it doesn't matter now. No one is here to get mad at us. I plan how Yo-Yo and I will survive.

Everything I see outside the window in front of me is melting behind a watery wall of thick and endless tears. My body tenses and shutters with every sob. I feel like I am floating away like a kite. The hand that tethers me to Yo-Yo is a string. Suddenly, I hear the phone ring. I tug Yo-Yo back to the kitchen. I let go of her to pull the wooden kitchen chair under the black phone on the wall so I can reach it. The receiver is heavy when I pick it up with two hands to listen. My Uncle Rod's voice says, "Bethie?" All I can do is cry and stutter. He continues, "Are you alone?" I can't find my words, but I hear, "I'll be right there!"

Yo-Yo stays in the house and I find myself waiting at the end of the walkway. Uncle Rod pulls up in his big car. I crawl across the cold vinyl seat beside him. Just above the dashboard, I see my father, a small silhouette framed in the windshield weaving its way up the hill toward our house on my brother's bicycle. My uncle and I wait. Dad tells us my mom took Nana to a doctor's appointment. A fire call came in so he responded to the firehouse like all available volunteer firefighters should. He forgot me.

Regardless of how many times family members tell this story, they laugh about it. I laugh along, but I can still feel the fear and anxiety of that childhood experience.

It's no surprise that food was one of the first things I thought about at that moment. In a household of chaos, our one anchor was food. Appointed mealtimes provided consistency and predictability. Celebrations like birthdays, holidays, weddings, and summer picnics evoked joy and were built around copious amounts of comfort food and sweets. Love looked like a kitchen counter full of three dazzling cookie jars filled with homemade cookies and a fresh-baked pie set in front of them. A warm Bundt cake with a sensuous drizzle of icing completed this altar of endearment.

Food soothed physical cravings and emotional hunger. Not all love is unconditional and my mother's expression of love came with a cost. Her usual reading post was at the kitchen table near her recently baked treats. When I went to take a cookie or a piece of pie or cake, without looking up from her book she would warn, "If you eat that you will get fat." My hand hovering over that sweet land of relief retreated. *Don't get fat! That's bad!* I learned to sneak into the kitchen, lift the cookie jar lid without a sound and steal as many cookies as I could at one time. I was freaking out that I'd get caught and thoroughly anxious with the anticipation of relief. Then I'd sneak out of sight and eat all of them at once so as not to get caught with the goods. All this love was right in front of me and it was emotionally and psychologically off-limits. Food was my anchor and my fear all at once.

When I was happy I ate for pleasure. When I was sad I ate to soothe pain. When I was stressed I ate to distract myself. Food was that one reliable thing that there was enough of, even when I felt *I* wasn't enough. I wasn't alone in this toxicity. All my siblings turned to food for comfort. It was the one addiction that we had in common. This made my actions all the more permissible, but I thought there was something different about me. My family regularly recited to me, "There once was a girl who had a little curl, right in the middle of her forehead…when she was good, she was very, very good…when she was bad, she was horrid." I did not know this was part of a poem. I thought they were describing me and I believed them.

The faulty core beliefs formed in childhood around circumstances like these became a silent, viral operating system in my brain on a constant loop: *I am a mistake. I am alone. I am unworthy. If I am perfect, I cannot be rejected or abandoned. If I hide, I am safe from judgment. Love is conditional.* These strong agreements would insidiously dominate my being for the next fifty years. In childhood, I learned to hide. I learned to solve my own problems with faulty reasoning. If I felt unsafe I sought approval or tried to numb my feelings. My distress showed up significantly in my relationship with food which became a confusing dance of cravings and relief.

When my older siblings became adults and left the house, my parents unleashed the official cold war between them. They weren't looking in my direction as long as my grades were good and I was home on time. At this time I became obsessed with body image: *if I look good, I* am *good.* My mother was a believer in laxatives. I learned that after using them I felt thinner, even if I couldn't be a size 0 or 2 like my friends. Diet pill use was an occasional thing for my mom so I accepted those as a normal part of "health" as well. By age sixteen, I discovered that partying and amphetamines were better at controlling hunger and losing weight. They were a hell of a lot more fun, too.

The sane moments during this rebellious time were when my two best friends and I cooked for each other. We would find ourselves away from the chaos of parties and having meaningless conversations over warm beer, and instead enjoying a main course of love and connection – the solution to our teenage angst. Thanks to my nana, I had always had a love and deep connection to gardening and preparing food. Cooking for friends made it easy to tap into this joy. It balanced the crazy paradox in my mind about food. I could de-stress and gain a semblance of peace and control.

Like a see-saw, the balance point shifted often. Binge or nourish? Purge or maintain? Am I good or am I bad? I believed I was always one or the other. The good girl hated the bad girl and the bad girl was at war with the good girl. They battled it out fiercely for supremacy in my subconscious. When chaos feels normal it's easy to get stuck in it. In my teens the bad girl controlled the chaos battlefield with poor decision-making and more distorted thinking. I went from a straight-A student to a delinquent with failing grades and near expulsion due to truancy; from talented athlete to party queen; from obedient daughter to wild child. I was too young and inexperienced to recognize these swings as signs of compulsive behavior that would deepen feelings of unworthiness and patterns of self-sabotage.

I found a safe place in my artwork. I loved painting and drawing; I was good at it and it gave me comfort. "You're such an artist! You should go to art school!" was added to the list of "shoulds" I heard from a very young age. I applied and got accepted to art school. I did extremely well and made honors. Until I didn't. My patterns hadn't changed. I invented the thought that the required critiques of my work were a reason to quit. The truth is, I was afraid of my success and afraid to shine. My mother's voice haunted me, *Do your best, but don't be a big shot. You will end up alone and no one will like you.*

During college, I was working full-time as a cocktail waitress in downtown Boston where the party scene never stopped. Work was an excuse to avoid classes. I left art school in my senior year without notice. I just never showed up again. Another attempt at full-time school at another college two years later ended similarly. If I wasn't running, I was hiding. Or both. I was in my early-twenties and I became a full-blown bulimic from stress and self-hate. The relentless voices in my head told me, *You'll never amount to anything. You are a failure.* The only things I graduated from were the occasional use of laxatives to vomiting at will. The part-time use of amphetamines became frequent use of cocaine. Poor impulse control often ended with remorse. "I'll never do *that* again!" was the magic phrase that almost guaranteed that I would do "that" again, and probably again and again. Whether it was the hangover that made me feel like shit, the drug use that left me spun out, the binging and purging that left me sicker and filled with more self-hatred, or the relationship that didn't work out and proved I was unlovable, I just traded one compulsive or self-destructive behavior for another. My parents often said to me, "If you're so smart, how can you be so stupid?" It was the question that I judged myself against. There must be something *really* wrong with me! My self-worth was based entirely on others' approval and acceptance. This drove me to over-achieve and seek success. At the same time, deep in my subconscious, an unhealed childhood belief was still running the show: *I am a mistake.*

The irony is that the deeper the spiral into self-destruction, the greater became my will to support and heal my body. How did I turn dust into gold? I studied herbalism, natural foods, and remedies, and delved deeper into plant-based nourishment. Knowledge and practice became my arsenal against the bad girl who was determined to keep me numb permanently. My environment changed, too. At thirty, I married. With loving stability and a feeling of acceptance, my eating disorder abated. After four years of marriage, we were granted a gift from Spirit: our son. His birth fostered an abundance of reasons to show up and shine. And I did. With all my heart. I was there for my family. I finished my college degree and took additional courses in plant-based education and raw food culinary arts. I built a nutritional coaching business and offered personal chef services. I was active, engaged, and happy. I was able to rewire my thoughts and feelings about food. I showed up as a higher version of myself. Until I didn't. Again! I simply re-enacted old stories in different ways. My relationship with food was under control, but my relationship with myself wasn't. The insidious subconscious belief that I am not good enough to exist, and the constant balancing act of good girl vs bad girl, was just waiting to crash the party because, deep down, I truly believed these things, and core beliefs don't just disappear unless hard work is done to change them.

My inner world eventually materialized in my relationship with my husband around money and my inability to set boundaries for myself and towards others. My husband and I made life choices that were the stuff dreams are made of. They also came with challenging consequences that I was unprepared to handle effectively because of many unhealed childhood beliefs. My fears created a wave of stress in me that rose up like a tsunami. Feeling completely out of control, I had traded my food compulsion for another. I spent more money than I earned. I panicked from fear of judgment and hid expenditures from my husband. I worked frantically to earn money. More money didn't change a thing. My husband threatened divorce if I did not get help and I did not want to be abandoned and alone. Shame and guilt were the judge and jury in my head. Self-worth plummeted to its deepest depth yet and condemned me with, *You'd be better off dead.* I had to dig deep to find the "good girl" in me to stay alive.

Relief came in an unexpected way. It wasn't food or drugs or alcohol or running away. To save my marriage I agreed to enter a recovery program that focused on debt. I went for my marriage and I stayed for myself. In this experience, I witnessed the strength and hope of others and I realized I was not alone in my compulsions and distorted thinking. My binary thinking of "I'm good" or I'm bad" pivoted into a sense of curiosity. The all or nothing habitual end points I set for myself softened.

Doing the work to discover my authentic self is a perpetual process. I'm learning that knowledge is power, but awareness is *powerful.* Awareness is a guiding point of light in the darkness. Willingness is a superpower for change. The seeds of self-acceptance create space for grace. I am willing to accept the mindset of *progress, not perfection.* Although I make mistakes, they do not define me.

My mother used to say, "You'll get your reward in heaven." I am learning to trust that the reward is right here, right now. This life is dynamic with pain and joy and curiosity and healing. Serenity is co-created with Spirit. All that is required of me is to show up with a willingness to change the things I can and the inner knowing that I am simply a human being, neither good nor bad.

PATH TO YOUR POWER

Here is a recipe for Soul Full Healing. This is a recipe to put in your toolbox of self-healing to nourish your self-worth and self-acceptance or when you want to quell the hunger pangs of fear, anger, or sadness in any or all of their forms. The power of this recipe is that *you* are the creator, the one who chooses what ingredients to include, how much to add, whether to blend, whisk, froth, or fold into your Being. The beauty of this recipe is that when we work on what's going on inside, we can change our world.

Serving Size: Individual
Preparation Time: Moment to Moment

Tools and Equipment

Self
Breath
Curiosity
Awareness
Willingness

Suggested Soul Full Ingredients

Choose one or add your own!

Acceptance, Love, Patience, Honesty, Accountability, Respect, Hope, Gratitude, Joy, Passion, Playfulness, Perspective, Creativity, Vulnerability, Receptivity, Objectivity,

Intuition, Reflection, Mindfulness

____

____

____

The Practice

Your Self is the vessel into which you will place your intention. Place yourself in calm and quiet surroundings. Using your Breath, prepare yourself by connecting to your breath to create inner space. Take ten slow, full belly breaths. Relax your body and slowly allow Curiosity to work with Breath. Ask yourself: *What compulsion am I struggling with?* In this present moment, let Awareness identify the compulsion. *What does this compulsion look like in my life? How is it showing up?* Then ask yourself: *What soul full nourishment will help my healing?*

Remaining in a state of Awareness, ask: *How does this nourishment feel in my body? What part(s) of my body need this nourishment the most?* With Willingness, allow the sensations to nourish every cell. Slowly savor its presence and allow it to come to full flavor. Incorporate the feeling. Sit gently with it and get to know it. Thank it for showing up. Store it in your body, your mind, and in your spirit and replenish and add ingredients as often as needed. Your soul full kitchen is always open.

ABOUT

Beth Nagle Griffin is a foodie and intuitive healer who guides and supports others on their journey to heal their personal relationship with food. With a Bachelor of Science in Art and Adult Learning, Raw Food Chef certification, and extensive studies in herbal and natural healing, Beth's wisdom is anchored in the energetics of plants and plant-based foods as well as nutritional science. By combining both, Beth believes we heal and grow holistically, and the ripple effect of healing reignites our sacred connection to food, to each other, and to the planet.

Beth also believes in the healing power of chocolate and handcrafts raw cacao confections with the highest vibrational ingredients. Soul Full Organic Chocolate, Beth's chocolate business, was created so that customers can explore the sensations of healing and indulging simultaneously all while enjoying decadently delicious, maple-sweetened creations.

Find out more about Beth, her services, and her delicious chocolate at www.bethnaglegriffin.com.

A MESSAGE FROM ALLYSON

You are what you tell yourself when no one else is around. You are what you do when no one is watching. You are the stories floating around in your head when you're doing mindless things such as cooking, driving, mowing the lawn, or taking a walk. That's who you are at your core. So, here's my question. Are you happy with that version of yourself?

It's not enough to read this book, or any book, in an effort to heal yourself. It's not enough to say you'll do better. The worst thing you can do is quit something for the next better thing like a new marriage, a new job, a new town – you get the picture.

What do you do when you're tired of being you? You change your narrative. You stop believing the bullshit stories you're telling yourself. You start understanding where your pain started. You heal that. You stop looking for approval and validation from others and start to understand that you do need those things, just not from other people. You need it from yourself.

Each of my clients comes to me wanting to feel better and usually to reach some outside goal, also, which usually includes having more money and/or more love. Those are great goals – fantastic goals, in fact. The thing is, those goals can't feel or look any different coming from the same place inside of you. Because, you see, what most people want is conditional happiness. What is that, you may ask? Allow me to explain.

If I/you (do the thing – lose weight, get married, get engaged, receive the raise) then I/you will be (happy, successful, wealthy, enough).

This way of living is exhausting! It's also defeating because there is never enough weight to lose, money to gain or love to experience that is going to make you feel like enough on the inside. Why? Because our worthiness is an inside job – not an outside/in job.

The bottom-line is simply this. Are you willing to decide that shame doesn't serve you? Are you willing to decide that your worth is non-negotiable? Are you willing to come to an agreement within yourself that you are worthy simply because you exist? If you're not willing, then your life is going to stay exactly the same that it is right now. It will only change according to what is happening on the outside of you–your job's condition, your spouse's mood, the economy–and that is a disempowering place of survival. It's the fastest way to find yourself in complete burnout.

The other option is a pathway. Before I explain how it works, I first want to share what it's not.

It's not toxic positivity where you're being super uplifting on the outside but still feel like crap on the inside. It's not spiritually bypassing where you're meditating, praying, and attending some type of spiritual/religious practice daily or weekly but still feel helpless and worthless on the inside. It's not reading affirmations, reciting them to and from work, but still believing that there's no hope for you. It's not waiting to be rescued by the perfect lover.

Here is how the pathway to empowerment works for those who are willing to step onto it. First, you must stay willing, even when things start to feel super scary, and that fear will happen. Second, it's being willing to journey into your past, find that hurt little person who was rejected, disowned, disillusioned, or powerless and healing that hurting heart. Third, stop comparing yourself to other people. Period.

Fourth, learn to trust yourself by taking calculated steps toward your goals. Fifth, come to understand that hurt people hurt people. It wasn't about you. Sixth, find a community of people where you feel safe, seen. and heard. This is going to go a long way in helping you step into your self-worth. Seventh, tap into your passions. If you love to paint, then paint. Passion doesn't always have to equate to dollars. Joy is priceless. Last but not least is number ten: learn self-compassion. You don't know what you don't know, so give yourself grace for mistakes you've made in your past, and pay that grace forward by coming to understand that failure, no matter how large or small, is part of life and learning.

If you abide by these ten steps on your journey to becoming empowered, you will start to understand that life isn't a straight line. You're going to go around in circles sometimes and that doesn't mean you're doing anything wrong or that you're crazy. It simply is an indication of your growth both personally and professionally.

If any or all of this resonates, please come into my circle by visiting www.allysonroberts.com. Here you will find a free meditation, registration for Painless Pivots to Power, and my contact information if you're ready to become Unapologetically Powerful through learning how the brain works, especially when you throw in a little bit of spirituality. You'll also be able to find out how to sign up for my annual live event – Behind the Power, and if you're interested in writing a chapter or an entire book, and being coached on how to show up in the world standing boldly in your power, that information is also available on my site.

Thank you for learning what's behind your power. I know the world is going to benefit from you finally stepping fully onto your powerful pathway.

ABOUT ALLYSON

Allyson Roberts knows what it takes to make it in this world. As a young woman who found herself homeless, pregnant, and forced to live in her car, she turned to the writing of Napoleon Hill for comfort and guidance. Little did she know then what a huge impact his philosophies would make in her life. As a cognitive-behavioral expert along with her natural intuition, Allyson has guided thousands of people all over the world to find their internal power.

From intimate one-on-one conversations to speaking at live events, Allyson uses her training to overcome trauma, childhood issues, self-worth struggles, and more. In her sessions, she utilizes her professional training, as well as her natural gifts and strategic life coaching experience to bring people from all walks of life to their unique purpose.

Allyson is the founder of Outrageous Freedom now known as Unapologetic Power, LLC, and best-selling programs such as the *Stop Shilting on Yourself, Painless Pivots to Power, and Unapologetic Power.* Her book, *The Spiritual Journey: The Part No One Talks about* is available through Amazon and Kindle.